BECOME A BUSINESS POWERHOUSE USING *feng shui*

How to 10x your results without working any harder

PATRICIA LOHAN

To my Dad,
My first entrepreneur role model.
Thank you for leading the way with your
creativity and big heart.
I love you.

CONTENTS

PREFACE

The power of one conversation and taking action.

The other night I sat between two of my friends here in Greece where we spend our summers. Just over a year ago, I was sitting between them both and it was a convo that changed my life forever.

The first told me stories of his life as a tennis pro in his twenties. I was so inspired by him and shared how I'd always loved watching tennis & out of my mouth popped - I'd love to learn tennis.

On the other side of me, my other friend told me about his mum winning tennis competitions across Africa when he was a child, how he'd played for years & out of his mouth popped - I could build a tennis court here. (we were at his house back then and this morning we all played tennis on his new court)

This tennis convo swirled around my head and I decided to go for it, with no idea of the consequences!!

I hired a coach and honestly have never looked back.

Putting this in context, I had never played any ball sports, I didn't know how to throw a ball so I was the worst 40 year old beginner ever!! My coach also realised I was afraid of the balls coming at me. No matter, I preserved (I'm still a total amateur)

Little did I know that I'd land on Necker Island (yes Richard Branson's Private Island) and find out that Richard played tennis twice a day, that he had a personal tennis coach we could train with and if we were any good we MIGHT get a chance to play with him.

All I knew was there was a tennis court & if we wanted to play bring our gear - a lofty laugh out loud comment I made was ohhh imagine if I get to play tennis with Richard Branson!! (AS IF)

The eager beaver newbie tennis player I signed up immediately to play with the tennis coach when offered with my friend Paige.

That night Richard came down to dinner and said he heard there were some tennis players, of course all the girls (fellow female entrepreneurs) knew it was me, and he invited us down to play in the morning at 6.30am.

Ok sure I said!!!!

I was SO nervous, I really wanted to pull out and wait until another day, I had never played a proper game EVER and was still crap, I knew I might never get this chance again. I just had to do it.

The next morning, Paige & I headed down, nervous excited and full of trepidation

We ended up having coffee with Richard and his coach. Richard actually made me tea, just the four of us, chatting about business, life and the universe, rolling around laughing at some of the pranks he has done on people until it was time to play.

He was so patient, kind and even helped me with my serve. My first official tennis match ever was with Richard Branson. We had two mornings like this with Richard. The first day it was a draw, the second I was Richard's partner and we won.

I had no idea what the trip to Necker would bring but that time spent with Richard was like GOLD to me. I learned so much just from our little chats it felt like such a gift.

Last night I realised it would never have happened if I hadn't followed that little nudge to start playing tennis. This is one of my favourite quotes from Steve Jobs that is exactly why following the nudges & taking action are so vital.

"You can't connect the dots looking forward. You can only connect them looking backward. So you have to trust that the dots will somehow connect in your future. You have to trust in something -- your gut, destiny, life, karma, whatever.

I believe and know we are always being guided from a higher place. I know for sure there is a reason you are holding this book in your hands. I hope the magic that has occurred as a result of embracing Feng Shui in my life and my business ripples far and wide into your life, business and home.

I was 30 when I came back from India, broke and unemployable. I'd gone there to find something I felt was missing and ended up having a massive spiritual awakening, after being invited to leave my parents' business (aka fired). Now I was back and living with my parents. I had just €50 in cash and a big loan to my name.

"What the hell am I doing with my life?" I thought as my mum poked her head around the bedroom door one morning and asked if I was still planning to go to the Christmas market in Dublin. I intended to go and sell all the stuff I had brought home with me from India — incense, sound bowls, artwork, you name it. In fact, the €50 was from my sister who had bought a €10 necklace from me and let me keep the €40 change because she knew I was broke.

I took my dad's old Jeep that had just enough fuel to get me to Dublin *(thankfully)*. Past the toll (and now down to €30), I had no idea how I was going to get home if this market didn't work out.

Thinking it might drum up some interest in the knick-knacks I was selling, I'd decided to host a free meditation sound bath across the road from the Christmas market before it began. Selling a few bits and bobs to earn enough money to get me home that evening turned into a jam-packed stall, the line three or four people deep, buying everything I had. My friend came to go for lunch with me and I ended up throwing her the keys to the jeep which I had parked illegally to move it for me. To my surprise I drove that old Jeep home with €2,000 in my pocket.

That €2,000 got me started. I made it through Christmas and had enough to buy presents. I got a nudge to move to Dublin and when I announced it, I didn't have a plan. Then one friend offered me her spare room rent-free. Another let me borrow her bicycle. I was sorted!. And so, I got to work building my holistic business whilst managing a yoga space. Some days I was earning as little as €5 a day, but I was working hard on myself and my business, reading self-help books, saying mantras, writing affirmations, and buying personal development courses.

I was incredibly happy. I had so much freedom every day, waking up wondering what was next. I had a deep desire to make a difference in the world, even though I wasn't sure how I would do that. I wanted to share the joy that I had connected with through yoga and sound healing in India along with earning more money and finding my soulmate.

I'd made a start, but I was impatient for more! My vision for my life was so much bigger, but I couldn't seem to figure out how to break through. I remember spending hours daydreaming and writing about my dreams. I'd grown up with entrepreneurial parents who worked all the time. As far back as I can remember, they ran restaurants, pubs, guesthouses, and hotels. I'd had a job since I was seven or eight. Business was what I knew but this was different; it felt like a vocation, it didn't feel like 'work'.

I was sooo happy, I was so grateful for everything and my energy focused solely showing gratitude for everything I did have, following the guidance and the signs I didn't even know were signs at the time! That's when incredible things started to happen and I realised how powerful *intention* could be.

I finally had enough money to get my own apartment and move out of the single box room in my friend's apartment. The day I moved in I said to my friend I'm not moving out of here until I'm moving in with my future husband, I can still see her roaring laughing at her but I was deadly serious. I realised that my apartment and especially my bedroom needed to support my current vision for my new love and business more intentionally. There was only one way I knew how to make that happen...

Feng Shui.

As a teenager, I loved Feng Shui. I was 15 when I received my first Feng Shui book as a gift. I even remember convincing my parents to hire a Feng Shui expert for their house and knowing deep down that, "Feng Shui is good for business".

I dug out those books and started implementing Feng Shui again, removing negative energy, setting up my space and bedroom for success. Determined to attract the right person, I Feng Shui-ed my bedroom for love. Soon after, I met Ken, my now-husband, and he told me he had Feng Shui-ed his bedroom for love too (the first time I visited I knew it). As coincidence upon coincidence came, I saw that Feng Shui was the answer especially when all my single friends were asking me HOW did you meet Ken?... I realised it was the missing piece of the manifesting puzzle for attracting what I truly wanted in all the other areas of my life.

I moved in with Ken and we dove into Feng Shui together. When the student is ready, the teacher appears, and not long after our decision to commit to learning all about it, two Feng Shui masters turned up in Ireland! Ken and I both knew we wanted to train with them.

As part of that training, our master did an analysis on our house and the first thing she asked was, "Ken, did you have financial difficulty last year?" My husband's jaw dropped and I nearly fell off my chair. She couldn't have known that Ken was self-employed, that his main contractor that year had not paid him for over six months or that he was on the verge of bankruptcy. She also couldn't have known that my holistic business had taken a hit too when I moved in. When that had happened, I'd told myself it was because I had moved to the countryside and all these other logical reasons as to why my business wasn't doing so well. Yet as we delved into the energy of our home with her, we discovered that the financial weirdness we had gone through was not our fault and could easily have been prevented and resolved.

Our house was in a money lock.

Later in this book, I'll explain exactly what this means. For now, suffice to say our money woes were resolved and they could have been avoided! Ken and I realised we needed to embrace Feng Shui fully. That day, we took the first step towards becoming official consultants in Feng Shui.

One night whilst cooking dinner we were discussing our honeymoon, contemplating a month-long honeymoon in India but we had both been there before and knew we needed more time to really enjoy it two, three or six months sounded better! This meant quitting everything, including my holistic business, which was pretty daunting — I was *the* singing bowl girl in Ireland, my business was doing great and had grown completely organically. Nevertheless, we rented out our house and I gave the online business thing a crack.

Looking back, I took some huge leaps. You definitely don't need to throw the baby out with the bathwater like I did! If I had sat back for five minutes, I could have figured out a way to transition my sound healing business online, selling singing bowls and setting up a shop. Instead, we went all-out. We packed up and moved. And we've sort of been on our honeymoon ever since!

After India, we went to Bali thinking we could rely on Ken's income while we were there, but the business he was working for didn't send him work and we only had a small rental income from our house. Still, we persisted knowing that something was going to happen. I had started my free Facebook group and was sharing videos of my life in Bali, answering questions about Feng Shui. That turned out to be the in-road for creating the PowerHouse Feng Shui online business that I'm known for today.

The best part about an online business is you don't have to invest a lot to get started. You just have to show up. The first time I ran my Feng Shui programme, six people joined. And I was ecstatic! It meant we could spend another month in Bali. That first six people turned into twelve, twelve to thirty-six, and that's when the fun started. Not just when I started seeing success, but when they did too.

Over time, blending my natural intuitive gifts, passion and the practices I've learnt as a healer and yoga teacher with Feng Shui, I have created the exact vision I had for my life back in that Dublin bedroom. I now live between homes across the world, as a *home-mad*, following the sun from Bali to Italy, Ireland to Greece. I travel the world with Ken and Toby (our adorable Bischon Frise) and I run a successful online business that I love and that makes a huge difference in the lives of my clients and community.

Nothing prepared me for the power of Feng Shui, I had NO idea the results and wins that were possible as a result of implementing Feng Shui. I started this from a place of fascination and curiosity but the transformations it has had on my life and business, and simultaneously for our clients' lives and businesses blow me away. Every day I'm in awe of this Alchemical practice that in so many ways doesn't make sense. This is what I intend to share with you in this book.

In *Become a Business Powerhouse with Feng Shui*, I will teach you how Feng Shui can be used in your business with easy, practical tips and real-life inspirational stories from myself and our clients. This is *the* beginner's guide to using Feng Shui for your business. You will start creating an office environment that is magnetic to your dreams and allows your business to soar to success.

If you've been where I was in those days in Dublin (dreaming big), if my story sounds anything like yours, this is the book for you. And even if you're not starting from scratch, if you've always had an interest in Feng Shui or you're an entrepreneur who wants to use all the resources available to you so that you can attain your vision for your life and business, this book will help you do that too. I'm going to tell you how to make that kind of magic happen, so you can have the impact you desire, touch the lives that you are here to transform, and bring the kind of abundance into your life that you deserve.

Feng Shui is a game-changer. It's where I learnt that everything starts at home. In the right environment, your dreams and intentions for your life can thrive and become your reality! And I'm so excited to be able to share this with you. You're about to start a journey that will enhance your office, your home, your business, your results, even your love life, in a way you've never seen before so you can live your dreams AWAKE.

It's time to make your home and workspace work for you. It is time to tap into using a resource you already have (your home) to bring in the success, abundance you desire. Your home is right there, waiting for that love and attention. It's ready to support you in your dreams.

Love, Patricia

INTRODUCTION

Feng Shui is not just about moving furniture, knocking down walls, hanging lucky trinkets or getting rid of mirrors. Okay, there's a bit of that, but it's not about superstition, 'hippie' peeps or 'woo woo' practices.

In fact, Feng Shui is used by big companies, major corporations, and many of the rich and famous around the world who want to improve their lives and businesses. Think Christian Dior, Oprah Winfrey, Madonna, Julia Roberts, Deepak Chopra and Tommy Hilfiger — to name a few!

Over 4,000 years old, Feng Shui is an ancient tool that originated in Eastern culture. I believe this is why it gets misunderstood in modern Western life. The reason Feng Shui is dismissed, particularly in business, is down to a lack of understanding of this ancient art. It wasn't originally designed for the way we live now. And yet Feng Shui can still work for you.

I like to describe Feng Shui as acupuncture for your home or office, as it uses the same Five Elements Theory as Traditional Chinese Medicine, Tai Chi, Qigong and Acupuncture. It's about working positively with the energy in your environment to enhance all aspects of your life and business. Feng Shui is like alchemy. It is magic at work. When we start working with our home, it changes us, our business, our alignment. We use it to balance that yin and yang energy to reach a centre point where energy moves smoothly and in alignment with the natural order of the Universe. This smooth energy flow is called *tao*. Reaching that point is what Feng Shui is about. Having your home, your business, and your life harmonised to the energetics around it so it feels like the place is supporting you, then tapping into that energy, magic and divine guidance too.

The irony of our lives in the modern day is that we spend most of our time and effort struggling to increase our abundance and then spend billions of dollars trying to improve our health. Feng Shui can support you to live and work with ease and flow, instead of hustle and grind.

I know, I know... we've been told success only comes with hard work! Well, my experience with Feng Shui would say otherwise.

Feng Shui centres around energy and flow. Just like you can't force the grass to grow or the flowers to bloom, we can open our lives and businesses to the natural rhythm and flow of the Universe. Like a river, when we move with this flow, it can allow more to happen for us faster because we're not in resistance. And to do that, we have to tend to ourselves, be of service and let *that* be the driving force of our businesses. It's a way of working that is different from the hustle and burnout culture we live in. (Believe me, I've been there too!)

Doing business with ease and joy can feel strange in today's reality, but it is doable and Feng Shui can support you in this way. If you can't sense it already, Feng Shui rocks my world and the world of my clients! Actually one of my clients has created a hashtag in our group #fengshuirocks

Let me tell you about one of those clients now.

Nina is a naturopath, whose work exploded once she started implementing Feng Shui in her home. She had been a naturopath and college lecturer for five years when she joined our PowerHouse programme. She lived and worked from her cute little home on the east coast of Australia that she loved. She was doing okay, but everything felt sluggish and she felt stuck. The business was just not moving forward even though her family life was super harmonious. If she wanted different results, she was going to have to do something different, and so she signed up for PowerHouse.

As part of the programme, she got her personalised Feng Shui report for her home and it revealed her home was great for people but not good for money. She implemented all the Feng Shui remedies recommended .

Things started to happen. The energy in the home shifted. And because she worked from home, all of a sudden Nina had this energy to show up and do her work. She wrote out a weekend programme from her zone of genius almost immediately and then ended up touring around seven cities teaching this work for weekend workshops. The money rolled in.

Even her husband's business started to flow! They'd always been okay, the bills had always been paid, but they had never had any extra money for all the other things they wanted. Suddenly they did, so Nina and her husband paid down their mortgage, bought an investment property, built an Airbnb, and created a legacy for their children.

All of these things came about because Nina decided to do the Feng Shui online course. She went from saying, "Who is this crazy energy lady talking about Feng Shui?" Aka Me!! LOL to seeing the results for herself.

When I asked her what she would tell others about using Feng Shui for their business, she said, "There's one thing that is absolutely undeniable. And that is your home, wherever that might be, is absolutely fundamental to everything. Everything stems from there. Everything, absolutely everything. Use your time wisely and intentionally to create what you want to create. The hours you spend applying Feng Shui to your home will be a magical time of transformation."

Of course, if you're 100% happy with everything in your life and business, then maybe you don't need Feng Shui. Maybe it's already working for you. But if you work hard to make improvements to your life and you're enthusiastic about positive change, there's no reason why you couldn't experience similar results to Nina.

Doing that will take a willingness to acknowledge the obstacles in your life and move on. It will take being honest and transparent about your situation and being willing to listen to suggestions and recommendations. You have to let go of what is not working for you and be open to receiving. Think about how energetically aligned your business is with your dream clients and also with your goals. Do incredible people just appear out of nowhere? Do you have the financial abundance and freedom that you desire? Do you feel supported and confident in your business?

When people ask me what 'bad Feng Shui' looks like, I ask them these questions: How's life? How's your Health? How's your business? How's your bank account? How's your life? Do your kids get on? Are things flowing happily and smoothly? What's going on in your life is an exact mirror of the energetics of your home and office. No matter what business you're in, balancing your environment is so important.

Maybe, like Nina, everything in your life is okay but just okay. It could be better. Who wouldn't want a business that was flourishing and thriving, rather than just getting by? Maybe you have a team that could be more in harmony with each other. Or you'd like a space that puts clients at ease when they visit you.

Feng Shui has the ability not only to stimulate your wealth sector and generate financial flow, but to improve your reputation, recognition, bring more balance and so much more. That has a positive ripple effect on everyone and everything in your life. (Especially if you work from home, Feng Shui will also harmonise everyone in the family!)

If you're in my world and reading this book, I know that you're someone who wants to help others, who wants to make a difference. You have something to share that you know needs to get out into the world. And if you're in the 0.01% that doesn't, it's likely that you haven't found *how* you want to help yet! You're here for a purpose. Whatever career you're in, whatever job you're doing, you are being of service and you're contributing to a better world.

Which is why this work is so important because it assists you in doing the life changing work you're doing. My business philosophy is all about helping people, being of support and of service. And I know, having seen it from thousands of clients, that Feng Shui can help you create a sacred space that supports you and your business. Supports you in shining your light in the world. Supports you in calling in abundance. Supports you in connecting with your divine purpose. This deserves to be a priority because your space is where you shine your light. This is where you do your soul's work.

It's time for you to shift into a new amazing era of your life.

An empowered, supportive space in your home and business can also boost your self-trust, enhance your relationships with clients, co-workers and others in your life, and increase your ability to attract money into your world. The best way to let money and success flow? Being at ease with your business and loving where you work, play and rest!

Don't worry, in all my years as a Feng Shui consultant, I've never once told anyone they've had to move house because of 'bad Feng Shui'. There are always things we can do to improve your environment and there are a million things you can focus on in Feng Shui to make it work for you.

It's time that we, as business owners and entrepreneurs, break through old patterns of lack. It's time that we bring our families and teams together into environments where everyone feels supported and nurtured. We have the ability to create a solid foundation to flourish in as well as lessen arguments, accidents and challenging behaviours. We can enhance the clarity, focus and direction of our business and our life pursuits to bring in more energy and abundance. Feng Shui helps with all of that.

It all starts, just like it did for me in that tiny box room in Dublin, with our intention.

What the hell am I doing with my life?

I ask you just that. What *are* you doing with your life? People build businesses for all sorts of reasons. Some do it for the money, some do it for the accolades, and some do it to help others. Some want to build a business that gives them more time for themselves. Some want to spend more time with their family. Everything I have ever trained in came from feeling a benefit from it (Reiki, Sound Healing, Feng Shui) and wanting to share that feeling with others which has led to me building a business that allows me to live according to my values of freedom and fun. Being clear on what success looks like for you is imperative to *holding the vision.* There's no 'right' or 'wrong' when it comes to success, only what you want to achieve.

When you combine your intention with what success looks like to you, it's like rocket fuel! I know from my own journey that the results we get for our clients in PowerHouse makes me think, "I have to keep doing this! More people need this!"

Holding yourself accountable to your intention and vision guides you through the tough times, particularly when you are trying something new and different. Plenty of the clients in my PowerHouse programme have had people in their lives who thought they were 'crazy' for trying Feng Shui remedies, but when it all starts to work... that's when people start asking, "So, what did you do?" Let your results do the talking.

Maybe you've tried Feng Shui before and it hasn't worked or you've implemented a few things and haven't noticed any results. You might feel reluctant to change anything in your home or office because there are others around or perhaps you feel afraid that you'll have to make big, structural changes. I want to set you straight with this guide.

I'm going to give you the easy changes you can do for yourself to implement to enhance your space. This book will show you how the basics of Feng Shui aren't those generic wishy-washy 'woo woo' things you may have heard, but that they are specific to you and your dreams.

The biggest and most important thing about Feng Shui is that each and every building, home or business has its own unique energetic blueprint. Just like our own date of birth and signature energy, your business (wherever you choose to run it from) has its own personality, history and imprint on the world too.

While I won't be able to go into the specifics of your own business or home here, it is something we do in the PowerHouse programme where we create a customised report for your home, sort of like a personal natal astrology chart that balances the invisible energy of your home.

In this book, I will share how I discover the story and energetic imprint of a space. This will give you the foundation to find the Feng Shui tools and intentional items to make your vision for your business come to life!

Getting your house, office and desk in order is a *must* for success in your business. And obviously, because your office and desk play a huge part in where you create from, connect from, and make money from, *Become a Business PowerHouse with Feng Shui* will go into the nitty-gritty of creating an office that sings success!

I'm so excited to share with you my top Feng Shui tips that are designed to spark joy, creativity and abundance in your business. At times you may wonder what the connection is between what I'm teaching and the practice of Feng Shui. I ask you to trust the process. Even a few basic practices can be incredibly powerful for your business.

Now that I've introduced you to why using Feng Shui in your business is important, here's what you can expect as we move through the Business PowerHouse book. This book is made up of five parts that take you through the simple Feng Shui techniques and how they can support your professional life, as well as your personal one.

In Part 1, I'll be sharing a little bit more of my story and *how* I uncovered its power in my business. I'll share its 4,000-year-old history with you, the different styles of Feng Shui, and why it still works for us today in this modern, fast-paced world. You'll assess your relationship with your business, office and home, and uncover what might be getting in the way of your business flourishing!

This leads us perfectly into Part 2, which is all about getting started with Feng Shui. I'll share how you can map out your home and/or office to create that all-important Feng Shui energetic foundation. Then we'll combine that with your assessment in Part 1 to start clearing out and letting go of the physical, mental and emotional roadblocks in your energetic space. Making space allows the Universe to fill us up with what we want (so long as we're being intentional), so you'll start to see real shifts here. One of my PowerHouse clients did the decluttering; then, after two years of her business going nowhere, she signed her first client!

Part 3 is all about practical Feng Shui enhancements that you can make intentionally for you and your business. We'll go through your home or office area by area, learning what each of the nine Power Centres represents and how to enhance each one for your business with intention.

In Part 4, we focus on the nitty-gritty of your office set-up, including chair and desk positioning, and decorations, and we even look at Feng Shui-ing your virtual home — your website. This is a super fun section where you get to amplify your energy and bring a renewed sense of purpose to your business space.

Finally, in Part 5, we look at the power of Feng Shui in your business. What to do when it looks like it's not working, how to hold your vision and intention when others stand in your way, the other obstacles that may come up for you, and what to continue working on once this book is finished.

Along the way, you'll find real-life stories from my PowerHouse members, like Nina's story from earlier in the book. One of my favourite parts of this process is the incredible transformations I see and hear in people's lives and businesses once they start to embrace this ancient art, so I wanted to include that as you embark on your Feng Shui journey too.

Like most things in business, those who step outside their comfort zone, implement Feng Shui to the highest level and go all-in are the ones who reap the most powerful rewards and transformations as a result. I hope they inspire you as we move through this together. If it can happen for them, it can happen for you.

It's all very well learning how to set up your office to attract money, or enhance your reputation, but knowing it and taking action on it are two different things. As I remind my clients in the PowerHouse course, you find 'action' in the word 'attraction' and that's no coincidence.

The journey you are about to go on allows you to take stock of where you are in business, as well as introducing you to a new awareness of what is possible when you embrace Feng Shui and start to dream even bigger. The steps are designed to help you create intentions and a space that complements your professional and personal goals, whether that be more money, clients, income streams, time, freedom, or even travel.

To be crystal clear about what to expect, this book is about making the first commitment to learning about this practice and applying it to your business. If you have dabbled in Feng Shui before, or seen tips online, then this is the perfect next step for you. Feng Shui has many elements and this book stops short of the personalisation that I teach in my signature course PowerHouse. For now, just sit back, relax, learn some Feng Shui basics, get comfortable with the energy of your home and office, and begin to understand it can support you. This will take you as far as you can possibly go without the personal assessment we do in our programme.

The last thing I want to mention is the PowerHouse Pauses and PowerHouse Practices that are threaded throughout the book. Within these pages, I have created space for you to pause, reflect and implement. These sections are potent, so don't skip them. The more intention you put into this, the more results you will get out. Your house is listening! I just got a message from a client who said just about everything I wrote about has come true so be careful what you wish for!

By the end of this book, it is my intention for you that you will know how to turn your office space into a place that attracts the success you envision for yourself. I hope it becomes a place of fun, creativity, joy and abundance... and that this becomes the familiar energy of your business and professional life moving forward.

POWERHOUSE PAUSE

Take some time to reflect and journal on these questions. You may even want to get a Feng Shui business journal or notepad specifically for anything that comes up as you work through the steps in this book.

Why did you start your business or get into the career you're in?

Why do you keep going?

What do you want to see in the world?

Where is the gap in the market that you fill in a way no one else does?

What are your business goals overall?

What are your business goals for the next quarter, next year, next five years?

What goals are you working on while you go through this book?

Getting clear on your intention is the first step to using Feng Shui in your life. You can't call in what you want unless you know what that is!

Download yourself a copy of my companion journaling guide from ***www.patricialohan.com/bizmiracles***

PART 1

WORKING WITH FENG SHUI IN YOUR BUSINESS

CHAPTER ONE
MY STORY

From 'Cry Day Friday' to Forbes...

My mum once fired me, she politely mentioned that she thought I should leave the business and out of my mouth popped - *I'm moving to India to become a yoga teacher(!!!!!)* everyone thought I was nuts (especially since my yoga experience had been a one hour class a week on a wednesday morning!) Not many people know that and it's a whole other story for a whole other book! Still, it's fair to say I've had my ups and downs in business. I had a burning passion for business, progress that came with having grown up with entrepreneurial parents. I liked material things and had all the glitz to prove it. My life was unbalanced and I was stuck in a life that looked great on the outside, but it wasn't my dream. I realised I was fulfilling my Dad's dream for him.

It was rough. I got sucked into the hustle, burnout, party culture. I worked like crazy and got caught up chasing shiny objects and partying. Designer dresses, shoes, bags, the nice apartment and the matching BMW parked outside. My life *looked* fab. I just didn't *feel* fab — no matter how I dressed it up. By the end of the week (every week). I would go home and cry uncontrollably on the couch, my boyfriend called it 'Cry Day Friday'. Literally. *That's* how bad it was. My soul was not happy.

Like many who find themselves in this state, it took a big change to set me on the right path. From my mum firing me to quitting everything and surrendering. I decided to step into my destiny and create a life I wanted for myself despite not knowing what that exactly looked like. When I moved to India to study as a yoga teacher, then came back and began my career as a holistic therapist, it was rooted in helping people release stress and anxiety from their lives. There was a lot of yoga, chanting, realisations and healing that took place, but in the midst of that, I had a spiritual awakening. I healed in a way I had never healed before. I changed my life by moving to India, changing my environment, now I help people change their lives by changing their environment without having to move to India!

Even though I had loved Feng Shui since I was gifted a book as a teenager, I'd assumed it was only for your home. When I picked it up again, I had no idea what was about to happen and how many areas of my life it would touch. After that first big success of calling in my husband Ken, the second was putting myself in service to wonderful women worldwide who now use my 'bag of Feng Shui tricks' to unlock this power in their own homes, businesses and relationships. As a by-product of all that, I've built multiple thriving businesses over the past 15 years, as well as having the freedom to do what I want, where I want, with the love of my life.

As I worked with my clients in my thriving holistic practice, they were doing 'all the things' but there was a missing piece, and I realised that their physical environment was impacting their lives and success. You know how they say you are the sum of the five people you spend the most time with? It's because of their energy! So, why wouldn't that be the case for your physical environment too?

And while there is nothing I'd change about my story now, there are some lessons I'd love to share with you. Here are the four things I wish I'd known before I got started on this path:

- **Your business can be full of ease and joy.** It can be so hard to swim against the tide and do things differently from everyone else when no one else can see your vision. When you allow yourself to relax into the flow, it will all come together as it's supposed to. Remember why you started your business. Then let it be easy. Maybe you will think, "Oh this is so simple it can't possibly work!" Often it is the simplest things that have the most profound results. Just try them and see.

- **You must stay true to your vision.** Everyone will have opinions and ideas on what you *should* do... but only you know, in your heart, what is right for you. I tell my PowerHouse members that they get to *live their dreams awake* and that their Feng Shui home can be their living, breathing vision board. That won't work without a vision! Feng Shui will help you anchor in these physical reminders so that you stay the course on this wild ride known as business.
- **Tend to yourself first to be of service to others.** You can't give from an empty cup, and actually, the more you give to yourself, the more helpful you will be to others too. As someone who did the hustle and burnout thing many times, I can't tell you the difference in the quality of results from overflowing with energy as opposed to hustling. And when you let this energy be the driving force behind your business, there's no stopping the flow.
- **Honour the divine timing.** Just like you can't force the grass to grow, you can't force your results. Pushing doesn't get you anywhere any faster... but removing roadblocks in your way can. It's why the first part of this book focuses on identifying those potential roadblocks in your life and business, and the second part focuses on clearing space physically, digitally and mentally. Only after that will we get to the intentional energy balances that Feng Shui provides.

Even when you think it's not working, I promise you it is! One of my PowerHouse clients said exactly this to me recently. "Just when I thought it wasn't working, a customer goes and puts in an early order this month *and* my husband comes home with a pay rise!"

I never set out to have a Feng Shui business or to help people live their dreams awake, but now I teach thousands of people every day how to tap into their innate power and turn their spaces, relationships and careers into supercharged magnets.

I could have never known that I'd go on to be featured in The New York Times, Cosmopolitan, Forbes, Huffington Post and USA Today to name a few. Or on television, radio and other digital media shows, including The Elaine Show. I've even been asked to speak at the Mind Body Spirit expos in Europe and Bali, among other live events, and interviewed for over 300 podcasts. When I launched my PowerHouse Feng Shui podcast, focusing on all things spiritual and holistic, it immediately went to the top of the Apple charts across the UK, Ireland and the US.

That girl who was once flogging her wares at a Dublin Christmas market has now gone on to build a collective community of over 68,000 people and gets a million sets of eyes on her website every year. It's fair to say I've learnt a lot over my last 15 years in business as my audience has grown with me.

As well as sharing with you the simple ways I got my business started with Feng Shui, I also want to impart the business knowledge and wisdom I have learnt over the years — in the hopes it will help someone else with their entrepreneurial journey. With my audience being all over the world, there will be something that applies to everyone in here, no matter where you work! After all, I am a digital nomad myself. (We like to call ourselves *home-mads*, because we have home bases all around the world.)

My journey has been a fun, hard, painful, exhilarating roller-coaster. My hope for you is that there's some knowledge in here that could make your journey a little easier. I've seen first-hand how women living their dream awake can have a wider impact in their lives and world, and I want to help spread that impact a little further.

Don't get me wrong, I still love nice stuff. I'm not immune to a beautiful bag or exquisite piece of artwork or jewellery. But now I can appreciate them for what they are and the energy they exude, instead of using them to fill a hole in my soul. I firmly believe that blessing needs to be shared. I want to give my knowledge, expertise and unique perspective on Feng Shui to you.

You don't need a dozen diplomas to make this work, although it's fine if you do. All you need is the willingness to get started. To listen. To implement. And to keep going, even when it looks like it's not working. Especially when it looks like it's not working. None of the Feng Shui teachings or business advice I'm about to share are hard. I don't believe in the hustle and grind of *hard.* I actually believe it can be easy and fun... but it is work. You have to be prepared to put in the effort and take the action. That's all I ask.

The magic, for me, started when I picked up a Feng Shui book. I'm hoping this book will do the same for you.

If you're ready to discover how your inner world, your mindset and your history completely affect your outer world environment and vice versa, and how you can work on them both simultaneously to achieve great things, you're in the right place. So, let's get started!

It's time to detox your business, unstick your beliefs, declutter your busy mind and get on the fast track to alignment with your dreams. It's time for you to get what you want from your business, be willing to take new and inspired action and see what your successful life looks like on the other side.

CHAPTER TWO

YOUR INTRODUCTION TO FENG SHUI

What is Feng Shui?

Feng Shui is a 4,000-year-old practice that is highly respected and considered a sacred practice in China. As I have seen in my life and business, and those of my clients, Feng Shui is a practical and tangible method for increasing abundance, health and wellbeing.

Feng means "wind" and *Shui* means "water". In Chinese culture, gentle wind and clear water have always been associated with good harvest and good health; thus, 'good Feng Shui' came to mean good livelihood and fortune, while 'bad Feng Shui' refers to hardship and misfortune. Who doesn't want a healthy, thriving business?

Feng Shui is the non-obvious reality of our environment. We are affected by things we cannot hear, see, smell, touch or taste. And yet, our five senses are involved in the experience of any given environment. We are affected physically, emotionally, socially and even financially by invisible energetic forces.

The relationship between Feng Shui and your business is much like the relationship you would or do have with a business partner. Some support each other; others challenge each other. It's about working together to create a harmonious and prosperous environment.

How a place feels will deeply affect a person's responses at both conscious and unconscious levels. While some places seem to feel naturally inviting, warm and inspiring, others do not feel quite right and people often will not thrive there, or worse, they want to leave quickly. Bringing Feng Shui into the internal and external design of a building can have immediate, noticeable, and positive effects on the way that people react and function there.

Types of Feng Shui

There are many different schools of Feng Shui; including Traditional or Classical, Black Hat Sect Tantric Buddhism, and Intuitive/Modern. There are variations in each school that account for various family lineage practices, which is why there is so much seemingly conflicting information out there.

I've had many clients come to me over the years claiming that Feng Shui didn't work for them. Since I know it *should* work, I've investigated what they have been doing. Usually, what has happened is they have Googled, "Feng Shui for offices", and got confusing results. It's not necessarily that what they've researched is wrong. Often, it is right, but wrong when used in a certain form.

The confusion comes down to the difference in mapping, a technique that you're going to learn properly in the next part of this book. Often, when you look up a Feng Shui plan online, Google will bring up a Feng Shui map for Western Feng Shui. The fact is Western Feng Shui was simplified and broken down in a generalised way for the West, making it much less effective. Western Feng Shui maps use the front door as the entry point. In Western Feng Shui, the entry point then dictates the locations of the different areas of your home.

Flying Stars Classical Feng Shui, on the other hand, uses compass directions to determine the different areas. For the purposes of this book, this is the style I will be sharing with you as I have seen the most success with it and find it much more accurate. We won't be going into the highly complex and technical layers in this book. We're still using the compass as a mapping tool for your home, just keeping it as simple as possible without losing the potency of it. Later, you will learn how to use the compass directions to map your office space and find all of the corresponding life areas so that you can make them more supportive in your life.

For now, I want you to put everything you have read, heard or know about Feng Shui in an imaginary box outside your door. Start this book with a blank canvas.

How Feng Shui can work for you

Most businesses in China will hire a Feng Shui consultant before a business consultant to see what's going on with their business. That's because Feng Shui is all about energy, or *chi.* In traditional Chinese medicine, every microcosm is thought to be made up of the five elements; metal, water, wood, fire and earth. Good health is achieved when the interactions between these elements cause the flow of your chi to occur in a smooth and balanced manner. By focusing on these elements in our space, we can reconnect with the natural order of things by bringing each element into balance. Like acupuncture, Feng Shui attempts to clear the 'stuck' energy and help the chi flow smoothly in your home/office and life.

So, what does that mean for your business? Once the energy is flowing as it should in your office space, here are just some of the potential results you can expect to see:

- A more profitable and successful business
- An office layout that maximises productivity
- Removing negative energy and friction between people and projects
- A more pleasant and harmonious working environment

- A reduction in employee turnover and sick days
- Finding the best location suitable to your business
- Giving your office the best possible good luck and success energy
- A thriving business!

If these claims sound unbelievable to you, I get it. I'm a Feng Shui consultant, so I am a little biased. You don't have to take my word for it though. Many businesses that you may recognise use Feng Shui. Heard of any of these? Whole Foods, Shangri-La Hotels, Nike, Intel, Bank of America, Hyundai. Yup, all of these businesses use Feng Shui to get a competitive edge. So, you're in good company.

Successful businesses use whatever tools they can to make them more successful. That's what you're doing here too. Let's get started then, by assessing what is currently working and not working in your business space.

Chapter Three

ASSESSING YOUR RELATIONSHIP WITH YOUR BUSINESS AND OFFICE

powerhouse [noun]
a person or thing of great energy, strength, or power

Being a person or having a business of great energy, strength, or power is the vision I hold for you. I want to help all women tap into the potential of their homes and thrive from that energy. So, how's that going for you so far? Now you've had a brief introduction to Feng Shui, it's time to assess the relationship between your business and your work space.

As I mentioned in the last chapter, there are lots more elements to Feng Shui. If you were to get a corporate Feng Shui consultation, for example, the consultant would take an existing building and maximise it to its full Feng Shui potential by looking at the floor plan, the power elements of employees, and the compass readings. From there, they can usually advise on the best area for HR to sit, or where the CEO's office should be, and they can often make all their recommendations without involving any renovations. These are all principles that you will begin to understand through this book, so you can get started Feng Shui-ing your own business.

Feng Shui consultants are often also used to help with relocations. So, when you are ready to move your business to a bigger site or expand operations to different locations, they help you screen your different options until you find the right location with the best Feng Shui for your business.

Of course, not everyone has office space for their business and many entrepreneurs work from home. This is still going to be a powerful exercise if you have your own home office or even if you work from your dining room table! Wherever you are, you want to work in an environment that is 100% supportive of you, your dreams and your vision for your business.

POWERHOUSE PRACTICE: Checking in with the space

Complete this questionnaire as best you can. There are no right or wrong answers. This is simply a starting point so you can see what your current working environment is reflecting back to you.

Download yourself a copy of the questionnaire in my companion journaling guide from ***www.patricialohan.com/bizmiracles***

Q1. Do you know the history of your home/office?

Q2. Since you've moved into your home/office, have you noticed any changes in your business either positive or negative?

Q3. Do you feel your home/office requires space-clearing or cleansing of old negative energy? (We'll get to how to do this in the next part!)

Q4. Is your home/office easy to find? Do clients visiting find it straightforward enough? Can the postman always deliver? Is parking an issue?

Q5. Have there been any large-scale extensions or remodelling done to your home/office? Have you noticed any changes since then? If you have, what changes did you notice?

Q6. What is going well with your business?

Q7. What is the temperature and lighting like in your office space?

Q8. What kind of music do you play in your office, if any?

Q9. Is there any soothing artwork?

Q10. How do you feel when you step into your office? Do your spirits rise or fall?

Q11. What are your favourite rooms/areas in your home/office? Why?

Q12. What are your least favourite rooms/areas in your home/ office? Why?

Q13. How do you feel about your business, your clients, your team?

Q14. What is your intention for your present home/office?

Our offices can be vessels that support, nurture and help us achieve our goals. Take some time to make your intention as clear as possible.

My overall intention for my business is:

Just reflecting on these questions, you might have some 'aha' moments or spot some red flags that you realise are not supporting you with good Feng Shui. Knowing the history is important because it can give you an indication of what may happen in the future. If previous owners or tenants did well in business or life, that's an amazing sign! If they didn't, bad history isn't a deal-breaker.

It's just helpful to be aware if you want to change the energy. Likewise, if people can't find you, if there isn't adequate signage or it's confusing when someone visits you, that means the chi can't get there either.

We'll get to how to improve these things soon! For now, this awareness is a great place to start.

About Your Business

On a scale of 1 to 5 with 1 being not at all and 5 being the most satisfied, choose the number that is appropriate for each of the following areas and questions. If the question is irrelevant to your business, feel free to skip it.

Relationships: Are you satisfied with your relationships with your clients and your team?

Career: Are you fulfilled in your business mission?

Mentors and networking: Do you have people to rely on for support?

Creativity: Do you have space and time for creative pursuits? Is your business always creating and evolving as you would like?

Fame and reputation: Is your business known as you would like it to be? Is your client base as big as you would like it to be?

Wealth: Are you satisfied with your financial situation?

Knowledge: Do you have adequate time for learning new things and nurturing yourself? Does your team have the opportunity to take time away from pressures during the day? Are there opportunities for your team to develop skills and knowledge?

Health: Do you have as much energy and vitality as you would like? Have you taken many sick days or time away from your business? How is the health of your team?

The core purpose of Feng Shui is to help you build a strong powerful connection that keeps you in flow. From your answers, you should start to see where your business may be out of alignment with your intention, and where your focus needs to be. As we move on, you'll see how each area of your business is reflected in a certain space too and what you can do to help align that energy externally so that you make forward progress in that area. You won't have to make radical changes to your office space. It is unbelievably easy to get started with Feng Shui in your business!

For now, I want you to take a few moments to imagine your business was your dream business, where you made the dream money, you worked the dream amount of time, and you had the dream clients. What would that all look like? Dream big. I once asked a client to think of the biggest, craziest dream number she could. She wrote it down and put it in her prosperity area. She went about her business, joined my PowerHouse programme when the time was right, and then got the £19 *million* she'd wanted. I can't make this stuff up! If that's not inspiration to dream big, I don't know what is.

I want you to think about what the most amazing scenario could be for each area of your life when we get to the nine sections of your home/office. If I had a magic wand, what would you want to happen? What would it look like? How would you feel? Who would you be?

If you want to invite *that* version in, you have to clear the space first. You have to acknowledge the crap that's happened, where you want to go, what you are doing with your business, how you want it to grow and what your dream vision for it would be. So, let's do that now.

Download yourself a copy of my companion journaling guide from to complete start to dream big :***www.patricialohan.com/bizmiracles***

JULIANA'S STORY:

"FENG SHUI WAS THE LAST PIECE OF THE JIGSAW FOR ME."

My husband and I were in business together. I'm also in business with my sister and my husband has a business of his own. We were struggling and there were a lot of areas in our lives that just weren't right because of it. Our relationship wasn't great and we blamed everything going wrong in our lives on the state of the businesses.

I decided to jump into Patricia's PowerHouse programme, even though my husband was the biggest sceptic and asked me how I proposed to pay for it. Nevertheless, I sorted out a plan and got to work.

Two months into the programme, we had put all the Feng Shui remedies in place and things started to change quickly in loads of areas. The main one was cash flow and my husband's career, so I was conscious of watching the career area and making sure everything was right. It was phenomenal for him! He'd taken a temporary contract with a company to bring in extra money as the businesses weren't providing enough, and after Christmas, they offered him a permanent position. He's now in a more senior role, getting double the money.

Fame and recognition was also an important area for us. The shop I run has been recognised for two years back to back. We've won bridal awards for our region and nationally! We also had a big shift with my son, who isn't struggling at school anymore. We became financially free from our mortgage at the turn of the Chinese New Year.

We've progressed so much. You don't realise how much until you actually sit down and make a list. People can see the change in us as a family too. We're just happier and everything seems to flow.

Before, there was always something with the business or money. Maybe somebody working for us wasn't pulling their weight. Now, all that friction is now gone. Feng Shui was the last piece of the jigsaw for me. Even my husband, the sceptic, is now 100% behind me with this... and his bonus paid for the PowerHouse course.

PART 2

GETTING STARTED WITH FENG SHUI

Chapter Four

DECLUTTERING AND MAKING SPACE

declutter [verb]
to remove unnecessary items from (an untidy or overcrowded place)

The first step to success in your business is to clear the clutter. This is a *must* for a happy, productive and successful business in all offices and homes.

If you want your business to grow and expand, it has to have space to do so! That's why, in this chapter, we are going to be doing both a physical and digital clear-out. We're going to look at your office, your desk, your storage systems and your filing.

This isn't just to make sure your business is all spick-and-span. Clutter has a huge mental drain on you. Not only can it increase your stress levels, but it also reduces focus and clarity. At home and in the office, people waste hours of valuable time each year searching for missing information or objects, or anguishing over messy surroundings. None of this is desirable in our businesses!

If you're feeling stuck professionally, creatively, spiritually or financially... it's likely there's some clutter in your space that's ready to go!

POWERHOUSE PAUSE

Before we begin this chapter, take a minute, close your eyes, and think about your office, your desk space, your laptop or wherever you work. This is the visual representation of your business. How does it feel?

If you are feeling overwhelmed, take a deep breath and look around at your office and desk space. What is there that is not necessary? Those things are currently blocking your creativity and flow in business.

POWERHOUSE PRACTICE: Set a decluttering intention

Ahead of decluttering, you'll need to set an intention. Here's why. If you aren't mindful, your home and office space will likely start to fill up with unhelpful junk again straight away. The items you have in your space are a mirror of your consciousness. As you begin to look closer, you will see what your subconscious has been calling in for you up to this point. I had one client who found a cushion that said 'f*ck off' in her prosperity area. What do you think happened when she wanted to call in money? It F....off!

If you want to stop your subconscious from sabotaging you, you need to be 100% clear on what you're welcoming into your home or office. Perhaps it's inspiration, clarity, or fun. Go back to that dream scenario you did at the end of the last chapter to give you some clear ideas on what you're calling in. Once you've set your intention, only things that energetically match what you want will remain or come into your home/office space.

What clutter should you be looking out for?

By clutter, I don't just mean an untidy desk. This isn't a tidy-up. This is a clear-out! Absolutely everything in your space is holding onto an energy and it's either helping or hurting you. And I want to bring to your attention that your office may need a spruce up.

First, declutter your desk. This will give you space to breathe and create. It's important to do this so that energy flows into your office and your business. Once you clear your desk, you'll feel the energy shift immediately. You might even feel your current stress and anxiety around your business immediately reduce. Having a neat and organised office honestly just makes such a big difference!

A clear desk invites more opportunities to land on it. (Watch out if you have a glass desk — glass represents opportunities coming and then vanishing! If you can, get a nice decal or table cloth to cover the glass. If you like, you could choose to switch to a wooden desk.)

Second, look out for anything symbolic. Some things might be in your energy field that you don't even realise are having an impact. I had one client who had legal issue paperwork stored in her desk that was a massive weight on her energy. Clear anything in your field that isn't bright, light, aligned, connected and visionary. Especially legal documentation! If you don't clear them away, they will continue to impact your energy every day.

Third, declutter your computer. Just like with your desk, if you have a busy digital desktop, you'll feel that overwhelm whenever you start your computer too. Clear your screen and take the time to go through your files, deleting anything you don't need, including old emails and contacts. Unsubscribe from newsletters you don't read. Get rid of anything you don't use right now in your business, unless you need to keep it for regulatory purposes. Don't avoid this just because you have an awful filing system in place or tonnes of old documents, ideas or paperwork relating to old businesses that you aren't even running anymore. If you're not obligated to keep digital documents, delete them and make space for new opportunities in your current business. If you do have to keep them for a certain time period, make sure they are stored away from your desktop.

Next, clear out other documents. You might have paper filing cabinets to declutter and paperwork that you need to archive too. Again, you may have legal and tax obligations requiring you to hang onto papers for a certain period. For example, in Ireland, where I'm a taxpayer and my business is registered, we have to keep our accounts for seven years. By all means, keep those ones. Beyond that? Shred. Use this opportunity to get organised and set aside only the specific things you need for your business. Declutter the rest.

One time, I had a conversation with a podcast host who said, "I keep saying this is the year I'm going to hit my goal, but it never happens. What would you say to someone who has been stuck for five years in business?" I asked her some questions about her home and she told me she hadn't changed anything in her office since moving in five years earlier. There were still boxes in the corner that she hadn't cleared out and this was directly affecting her career. It's time to clear stuff that is stuck and creating unknown stagnancy in your business!

Clearing out your computer files and documents is so powerful. Once you know where everything is, it can help you feel more in control and more on top of your business because you're not having to sift through everything. Think of it as a factory reset.

One last tip for documentation. Don't put files *too* far out of sight, such as in the attic. That's going to create an overwhelming stretching sensation like you've spread yourself too thin. We're trying to avoid that feeling!

Bottom line: keep anything you need, give everything a home, and get rid of anything that is not in alignment with where you are going in your business.

Colour code your files

Organising your files is a huge advantage in Feng Shui terms, especially when you colour code your system. Once you've decluttered, using colours to manifest and amplify more of what you want is a great thing to do. And it goes hand in hand with decluttering and then tidying up. In this section, I'm going to go through the power of colours for different areas so that you can use it to create and attract more business.

Client information: Green represents growth in Feng Shui. Think of the colour of trees and plants and what that represents. Put your current client information into green folders.

Prospective clients: In Feng Shui, red represents fire. If you intend to convert potential clients into new clients, you'll want to bring the fire! Red is energising, so I recommend putting the information of any prospective clients that you're talking to and leads you think are interested in you or your services into a red folder. Red will also allow the prospect to feel more urgency around becoming one of your actual clients. Even if you aren't sure about a prospect, still put them in your red folder as it will help make them more magnetic to you.

Creative projects: Purple is the colour of magicians, magic and manifesting. It's an amazing colour for whatever you want to *attract*. If you want to manifest something new in your business, I would suggest putting it in a purple folder. Let's say, for example, you have a new business idea, or you want to do something a little bit different. Put all your notes, research and the information you've gathered into a purple folder.

Investments and banking information: It's likely you want your investments to rise and grow, so red or green folders work for these too. If your focus is increasing and bringing fire energy into your bank account, go for red. If you want to nurture your investments and watch them grow over time, choose green.

Bills and legal issues: Blue represents the water element. It is a dampener, a cooler. Black is on the same colour chart as blue. If you want to reduce your bills and monthly outgoings, give blue or black folders a try.

For any of your business areas, you can write affirmations and place them inside the appropriate folder to make your intentions more magnetic.

Keeping books in your office

Just like filing cabinets, bookcases become overfilled. You might think that anything tucked away on a shelf or in a box doesn't affect the chi, but having storage doesn't mean the contents are organised, clear or supportive. It's time to declutter your bookshelves too.

Believe me, I know this one is hard. In our home in Ireland, Ken and I had four *huge* bookcases. They were filled with books we, admittedly, were never going to read again.

Letting go of books is usually the hardest part of decluttering. Your ego may be saying, "But look at my well-read bookshelf!" or "I'm definitely going to read that again someday." Be honest with yourself. Are you going to read that book again? Could that information better serve someone else? Give books away to people who will read them. Share the knowledge around! Clearing your shelves allows you to create space for new information and insights.

I had one client who moved into a home with the original bookshelves — and the books! Thirty-two years, those books had been there. Imagine the stagnancy of all that information reflecting back into her business!

Is everything light, bright and working properly?

Decluttering and dim lighting go hand in hand. Lighting is often dingy in cluttered crowded cupboards that are full of things you don't need. In those places where you can never find what you're looking for, doing something about dim lighting is part of the decluttering process.

It's important that our environment supports us and full-spectrum lighting maximises that. You'll need to make sure your office or the spot where you have your desk has as much full-spectrum light as possible. Light is energising, so it brings fresh energy in our business.

Be mindful and have a look around. Is the area where you work as bright as it possibly can be? Can you bring in a lamp or light it up some other way? Do you need to replace any broken light bulbs or dust the working ones? Are the lighting bars on your laptop working? Burnt-out light bulbs represent being burnt-out, so make sure you address this. Clean your office windows too.

You might even go one step further and make sure all the lighting on your electrical equipment is adjusted for eye comfort at different light levels of the day — most computers have this functionality built-in now. Anything that helps you see better will also support you and your business to thrive.

Beyond burnt-out lightbulbs, anything broken needs to go. Handles, in particular, represent your grip on your finances and your grip on life. If there are any friction points in your home or office, anything that's creaky or not flowing easily, anything that jams, these sticking points are reflected in your energy system and back into your home. Make sure you fix anything that's bothering you!

Are you inspired by what's in your office?

Take a look around now and make sure that the items left in your office are comfortable and inspiring to you. Your workspace should be your source of inspiration, a place that you get energy from just by being in it. Inspiration almost always goes hand in hand with productivity, which is why it's so important that your environment mirrors that.

Where you work should look the way you want your business to look, because your business is a reflection of the environment it lives in. If you run a health food company, for example, but your office has junk food wrappers everywhere, that's not exactly aligned! Anything that doesn't match your intention, reflect your business, or inspire you, needs to go.

Maximise the space you have

There are a few other things to look for in a space. Low ceilings and beams create the idea of extra pressure on your shoulders and hinder progress in your business. If you were choosing your office building from scratch, it would be helpful to look for something with a higher ceiling and where you don't have to sit under beams.

Of course, many people won't have the luxury of renting a new office or picking their ceiling height, so decluttering is the tool to use for maximising the space you do have. We'll also talk about this in the section on desk positioning later in the book.

A good declutter and keeping your desk clear every day will keep the energy fresh and rejuvenated. Emptying the rubbish bins every day is another good way to declutter too. Decluttering is futile if you allow it to all build up again, so it's about creating a regular practice of clearing and letting go what doesn't serve you and your business.

While this may sound counterintuitive, adding in plants or flowers contributes to a feeling of spaciousness too. Plants are great because they put oxygen into your office. More oxygen means more fresh energy in your body, which means feeling more invigorated and being able to do what you want to do in your business. Later, we will explore more what you can add in to feel uplifted, bright and inspired, but let's stick with removing and clearing for now!

If there are distractions like exercise equipment or children's toys in your office, your energy will dissipate. It needs to be centred on where you're going and what you want to achieve in your business, so remove anything causing you to be unfocussed.

Clear out under your desk too, as this represents under-the-surface emotions and stuff that you need to bring up and let go. What else do you have an excess of that you're never going to need? Pens? Sticky notes? Time to go!

Desk, computer, documents, lighting, books and broken items — those six simple focus areas will help you get started organising your office space and welcoming fresh energy into your business. What we're doing here is creating a space that is supportive of you, of what you want to attract, and of a business that feels incredible.

POWERHOUSE PRACTICE: Complete your decluttering

What can you declutter?

- Paperwork and old documents (including old businesses, bills, receipts, appraisal forms, and bank statements).

- Books (if you've read them already — are you going to read them again?).
- Equipment and stationery that you no longer use.
- Anything broken!
- Anything unrelated to building your empire that causes a distraction e.g. exercise equipment, children's toys, suitcases.

Do a digital declutter:

- Keep your screen clear (perhaps put your vision board on it as your desktop picture).
- Get rid of unwanted files on your computer.
- Delete emails and unwanted email addresses.
- Use Unroll.me to unsubscribe from emails.

Other decluttering tasks to complete:

- Organise and colour code your files.
- Clean and dust your office space (including cleaning the windows, dusting the lampshades... etc.).
- Commit to doing a deep clean for even better results!
- Maximise your space by moving around furniture if you can (we'll get to the best positioning of furniture later on in the book).
- Get some plants for fresh oxygen in your office space.

Be mindful as you complete these tasks. Start looking at your business with a fresh perspective and get rid of anything that doesn't belong in your workspace or your world.

As you begin this process and start to clear your clutter, you might start to notice how much lighter and happier you become. You might feel yourself shift out of that funk or rut you've been in. You might get energy seemingly out of nowhere and your business momentum might skyrocket! I know I've certainly seen that with many of my clients in the PowerHouse programme who have committed to decluttering.

Not only does this process create space for new possibilities, opportunities and ideas, but also it often helps you become clear-headed, focused and insightful. When you are clear, you have greater confidence in your abilities and decisions for your business, which also makes you feel more hopeful and optimistic about the future.

And once you embody that energy, the Universe can't help but send more of that to you! Being a vibrational match for what you want is the easiest way to let it flow right through your office door and straight to you!

More than just attracting new clients and added abundance, think of how all that organisation is going to revitalise your business, how much time you're going to save knowing where everything is, how much certainty you'll have about what to do next, and being able to manage your daily business tasks easily and effortlessly.

Decluttering is a never-ending process, and I know it can feel like one extra thing to do in your already busy business. However, removing distracting clutter will free up that time, giving you clarity about what you should focus on and forward momentum. It's like an audit for your physical space. The more you do it, the easier it is to let go and release.

If you're struggling to let go of some items, here are a few last practical tips to kickstart your decluttering.

Three-box method

Get three boxes to put your stuff into and label them: 'keep', 'maybe', and 'get rid of'. If you can't find a box, you could also make piles.

When you look at each item, if your thoughts are something like, "I'm definitely keeping that", it goes on the 'keep' pile. If you think, "I'm definitely getting rid of that", that's easy too! Into the 'get rid of' box and onto the next item. By the end, you'll know what you're getting rid of and what you're keeping.

The 'maybe' pile is everything you're not ready to part with but are unsure you want to keep. You can come back to it when you have the energy to go through it again.

Embrace giving

Everything in the 'get rid of' box can go to a charity shop, to recycling, or even for sale on eBay. There are so many good ways to let go of different items. You may even make some money or be able to give some of your stuff to a better cause.

For books in particular, you can think of giving them away as an energetic exchange. As you're packing up the books for donation, say to each one, "Thank you for the information you've provided me with. I'm now exchanging you for 10 new clients I can practice that knowledge on."

Come back later

You may have to wait a while before you tackle the 'maybe' pile. Usually, I leave those items in a box. Then, if I haven't looked for those items within two weeks, I know I haven't been using them regularly. That's when I go back to the box and try to guess what's in it. If I can't remember, I must be hanging onto that stuff for some unknown reason. If I have no idea what that reason is, I get rid of it.

Partner up

You might choose to work with a business buddy or assistant who is clear on saying 'yes' or 'no' on the items you keep or discard. Take the 'maybe' box and hold up each item to them. Yes, no, no, yes, no, yes, yes. Just like that.

For me, that person is usually Ken. He'll say, "No, get rid of it. I hate it. I'm sick of looking at it. That always breaks. That doesn't look right anymore." Or he might go, "We can use that for an upcoming course. Keep it."

Do this for everything in your office that you put into the 'maybe' box.

Inch it out

There might be stuff that you know deep in your heart needs to go, but you're not quite ready to get rid of it. For example, let's say you find the first set of business cards you ever made. They're nostalgic about how far you've come, but they don't represent where you are now or where you're going in business. You're never going to hand them out again and they are preventing you from moving on. It's like you've got one foot in that old career and you're not fully aligned.

Items like this go in a box or bag that you then place by the door. As items move physically closer to the door, you are closer to letting them go energetically. In a few months' time, when you want to clear out more space and get rid of that bag, you'll probably look inside and go, "These old things? Throw them out!"

AMBER'S STORY:
"IMMEDIATELY I HAD A CLIENT SIGN ON THE SPOT."

I'd done another Feng Shui programme before and I found it useful, but I didn't see any drastic changes. So, you can imagine my husband's delight when I said, "Oh, here's another Feng Shui course I want to do."

Immediately after sweeping outside the front door and doing as Patricia recommended, I had a client sign on the spot for a website build. Normally, with a website build, you have to do a proposal and they discuss it with you, and you go through all that process. But no, this client just wanted to go straight ahead and do it. Then, the second time around, after cleaning the front door, the same thing happened. It was exactly what I wrote in my affirmations, "I'm getting more and more ideal clients."

Then, I wanted to do a training course that cost $1,000. I left it to the Universe. "If it's meant to be it's meant to be", I thought. About two weeks later, I received an email and the course was on offer as part of a 25-course package for $99! Not only would I get access to 24 other business courses and the one I want was included too, but also it was only $99 rather than $999. I was blown away. I could never have guessed something like that would happen.

It took days to see all the noticeable changes from doing PowerHouse. More money is flowing in so much easier, not just a few dollars and like everything I've asked for is happening! The health of my kids and their relationship is improving which has been priceless. My job. My family. Even my relationship with my brother has improved.

Chapter Five

MENTALLY AND EMOTIONALLY MAKING SPACE

Decluttering is great for the energy and space it gives you emotionally, but the reverse is also true. If you still find it tough to get rid of particular items because you don't feel ready, you may need to deal with the emotions behind letting go of them first.

Sacred Space Clearing

An energetic declutter is so powerful and profound, and it's something you can do whenever something in your home/office feels a little off. This is one of my favourite practices. It's called Sacred Space Clearing. (Don't be put off by the word 'sacred'. Doing it the way I'm going to teach you will introduce a lightness as you move around your home/office. There's also an accompanying meditation to do alongside the practice.)

So, what is Sacred Space Clearing? This is a ritual you can use to clear a layer of negative energy that could be hanging around your home/

office. It's another form of decluttering, but this is for the energy you can't see.

When you want to do a Sacred Space Clearing, the first thing to do is select your tools of choice. They could be:

- A clearing tool that uses sound (Tibetan bowls, gongs, bells, chimes). Sound shifts energy the same way loud drumming vibrates through your body. Even a saucepan and wooden spoon, clapping or singing would do the trick. You could also download a Tibetan bowl audio. Essentially, sound will permeate the cells of your house or office, feel the stagnant energy and shake it out.
- Smudge sticks such as white sage bundles (not the cooking kind but the type you find in holistic stores) or palo santo sticks (wood from South America that you burn). You can also use incense, but I've found it's not as effective.
- Rosewater. This isn't a necessity but it is a lovely addition to the process.

There are no hard or fast rules on what to use. You can use one clearing tool of your choice or more. I'm simply sharing a sequence that has worked for me over the years. And if you're reading this and imagining your family will think you're bonkers, maybe wait until they've all gone out to do this Sacred Space Clearing!

The next step is to open all the windows. As you start clearing the energy, you want it to leave. You don't want it to settle back in around your home or office! If it's super cold, slightly opening one window will still work energetically and intentionally. You simply need a place to send out the negative energy.

Then, before you begin, protect yourself energetically and intentionally so you aren't absorbing into your energy field any of the energy that you are clearing. Even if it sounds weird right now, I highly recommend taking one minute before you do anything to close your eyes and imagine a bubble of light around you.

Here's how you can do that.

MEDITATION: Protecting your energy before a Sacred Space Clearing

Close your eyes and connect to the earth. Imagine growing roots from your feet that sink all the way down into the ground. Then picture a beam of light flowing from the sky into the crown of your head.

You're now in a channel of light. Imagine that light expanding and becoming a bubble of light around you. On the outside of that bubble of light, imagine that it's reflective or mirrored. The outside of the bubble will reflect away any energy you move around the house. As you move the energy out of the house, the reflective bubble will protect you from absorbing anything into your energy field.

At this moment, drop into your heart, and connect with what your intentions are for your home, office and business. Whatever you want to call in, whatever you welcome, be clear and allow it to be a mantra or intention that you repeat to yourself while clearing.

Now, we begin.

POWERHOUSE PRACTICE: Performing a Sacred Space Clearing ritual

Start at your front door or the door to your office. Using the bowl, music, smudging stick or clearing tool, move around your house/ office clockwise. Go into every little corner, behind the couches, into the places you haven't been in ages, into the cupboards you never open, into all the spaces. Take the sounds or smoke with you and cleanse all these spaces.

As you move around, you might see more smoke coming from the sage or palo santo or hear the bell sounding different. This often happens with smudge sticks and singing bowls as you move and change places. It is absolutely amazing how they can become so different, sound so different, depending where you go!

If the singing bowl feels heavy or the sound isn't as clear in some areas, increase the sound in that area. Clap your hands or sing a song that you love. Allow that sound to permeate through. You will feel a shift.

If you're doing this ritual with singing bowls or song, you can then repeat the process with smudge sticks. Once you have finished smudging, you can spritz rosewater around to bring sweetness into the space and fill it with the essence of rose. Afterwards, I recommend having a shower to wash away anything that came up and even spending some time outside in nature to ground yourself.

This Sacred Space Clearing is powerful. I remember doing one for a client's restaurant business and the next morning new customers walked in. The restaurant had been open for three years, but the customers who came in that day asked if the restaurant was new because they had never noticed it before. It was as if a layer had been removed from the building and it was being seen for the first time.

You can download the audio to use in the background for the Space Clearing of Tibetan Bowls I recorded for you here **www.patricialohan.com/bizmiracles**

Release past stories

Now that you've cleared out that energy, it's time to dissolve the negative energies stored in your auric field too. Many of us have negative memories about our business that make us scared of repeating things that we don't want to happen. These can be subconscious, but they can still hold us back. These negative business beliefs are blocking the flow of energy within us.

What are some things that you are afraid of happening or that have happened in the past and you are afraid of repeating?

In my own business, I had a period where I had this weird energy around Facebook ads. There had been a few comments on my ads saying things like Feng Shui was the work of the devil and that Jesus would save me. Even though I knew this was just part of the business being seen, when I became better known and more successful, these comments threw my energy for a while. Then one day, our account was completely shut down!

Before the account would be reactivated, I knew I would have to journal about those negative thoughts, feelings, emotions and beliefs — to get grateful for what Facebook ads were doing for my business. So, I sat down with Ken and wrote a list of all the amazing things that had happened with Facebook so we could change the energy around it. I wrote about how my free Facebook group allowed me to build an amazing community when no one knew who I was. I wrote about how my testimonials always included how I pop up on people's Facebook feeds randomly and how my programme then transformed their lives. I wrote about my gratitude for a platform that I could pay to put me in front of the people who needed me. And it worked!

It's all about energy. The most important thing is waking up every morning and thinking about the positive impact that your business is having on the world. Sometimes it's a simple reframe. If you believe Facebook ads aren't going to work for you, they won't! If you're creating all this negative energy around them, you need to find a way to change your perspective on it.

Years ago, Ken was pretty miserable at his job. Ken now works with me in our business and runs it all (He is the best). Back when he was a draughtsman, though, he used to complain to me about his work. One day, I asked him what he was working on and he said it was a water treatment plant in Sudan. I said to him, "Wow! Do you realise how important that job is? The impact that is going to have on the people in Sudan? The difference it will make for people who need clean water and don't have it? Your skills are setting the ball in motion for thousands if not millions of people to have clean water."

When you are holding resentment for something, but can reframe it in this way, you can alchemise that negative energy into a positive force for good.

POWERHOUSE PRACTICE:
Reframe your resentments

Take your journal and write out all the memories and past stories you have around your business while you've been in your current home/office. Anything that comes up that you want to release, write it down. Anything you remember as a particularly happy moment, write that down as well. And anything you know about the previous owners or residents in the house, write that down too. If you don't know of any experiences that went on in your house before you lived there, just write down what you do know from your time there.

Download yourself a copy of the prompts in my companion journaling guide from ***www.patricialohan.com/bizmiracles***

Here are some prompts to help the memories flow:

- Anything traumatic
- Anything emotional
- Anything that caused anxiety or stress
- Interactions with clients
- Interactions with friends
- Interactions with family
- Interactions with your partner
- Arguments
- Something breaking
- Something upsetting you
- Times you upset someone else
- Times you received bad news or a bad testimonial
- Stories or rumours about past owners

Allow the memories to come up and flow out onto the paper without judgement or overthinking. If it's a memory within you, it is a memory still in the walls of your house/office that needs to be released. By committing it to paper, you begin to release the memory from your energy system.

Note: This process will have an impact on your energy system, the energy systems of everybody who lives with you, and the energy system of your home/office itself. While your home will become your best friend in the long run by releasing all these memories, this process can leave you depleted in the short term. You may feel tired after doing this part of the exercise. You may also feel huge resistance to sitting down and doing it. If either of these is the case, know that it is completely natural. Be gentle with yourself. Take a break. Sit outside and take a few breaths or go out for a walk, then come back to it.

Once you have your list, go through the negative memories one by one and consciously decide to let go of each one. To do this, look at the memory and ask aloud, "Do I want to let go of this?" Then answer aloud, "Yes, I do." Alternatively, you can ask yourself, "Am I ready to release this memory now?" And you would respond, "Yes, I am ready to release this now."

After you have gone through each and every one of the memories, put them into a small fire-proof container and burn the pages. Please take care doing this and make sure you stay safe. I recommend doing this outside if you can or throwing the pages into a lit fireplace if you have one. If not, I suggest a metal dish for burning the pages, then washing the ashes down the sink or toilet with running water. If it's not safe to burn them, just tear them up and put them in the bin.

As you burn or shred the negative memories, you honour your business by completely letting go of all that has been held inside your energy system and the energy system of your home/office.

With the physical release of those burnt or binned pages, you may feel an emotional release. If you feel the need to cry when anything comes up, it's okay to shed some tears. Remember, you may have been holding this inside for quite some time. You might feel you want to get rid of these memories quickly, but be gentle with yourself. Afterwards, I recommend going out into the fresh air, even going out barefoot onto some grass if you can, taking some more deep breaths, going for a walk, and allowing yourself to feel cleared of the past. Drink plenty of water to support your body too.

MEDITATION: Connect with the soul of your space

Now that you've removed the old energy from your home/office and acknowledged the negative memories within you to be released, you can reconnect with the soul of your home/office. Use this meditation to truly connect with the vision you hold for yourself, your future and your business. Dig deep into what that dream life looks like for you, your family and the life you will create in this home.

Download yourself the meditation I've recorded for you from ***www.patricialohan.com/bizmiracles***

Get into a comfortable position, sitting or lying down. Relax your shoulders and settle in. Come into your breath and into your body. Let go of the day, any thoughts floating across your mind. Give yourself permission to relax completely.

In this relaxed space, connect with the heavens above, the universal life force energy, and the Mother Creator, the heart of Mother Earth. Imagine a beautiful beam of light glowing down onto the crown of your head. This light is an unlimited supply of energy, washing over your body, cleansing, healing, clearing, and releasing anything that is in not alignment with its high vibration of powerful love.

Allow the light now to filter down through your body. Through your crown, through your third eye. Through the forehead, the eyes, the nose, the cheeks. Allow that light to flood down through the neck, the throat, the shoulders. Release any tension across the back. Feel your entire body being illuminated.

Allow the light to flood down the spine now, the heart, the lungs, the chest. Down into the solar plexus, your organs, both arms, and out through the fingertips. It illuminates and cleanses any darkness. The light pours down into the root chakra, and all the way down through the hips, the legs, the knees, the ankles. This energy moves down through the feet, all the way into Mother Earth.

As it breaks through the soil, it moves down through the layers of the Earth, all the way down into this fire energy at the core, the colour of passion, the centre of Mother Earth. The white light that's pouring all the way down through us meets the core of the Earth, where all is made manifest and brought to reality.

Now, this red energy starts to move all the way back up through the channel created, all the way up through your feet, ankles, legs, hips, bringing this fire energy from Mother Earth.

At the heart centre, this infinite fire energy from the earth and the white light from the heavens become one. As these two colours mingle together, it creates a gorgeous pink light, the colour of pure, unconditional love. Your entire body resonates with this energy of unconditional love and you allow it to fill your entire body and extend it out until there's a bubble of pink energy all around you.

From this space of unconditional love, connect with your intention for your home, your office, your business. From your heart, allow these feelings of love, joy, peace, happiness, abundance, success, ease and flow to flow like a river around your house, flowing out of your heart into the room that you're in now, into the furniture, into the walls, into the artwork. Allow it to enter every space in your home, each nook and cranny, all the corners and crevices.

Feel the energy of your home now absorbing these intentions. As you move through each and every room in your mind's eye, feel the continuous flow from your heart moving into the bedrooms, and the kitchen, and the living room, the dining area, the bathrooms, the entrance, so the entire home is now filled with this powerful unconditional love energy.

Allow yourself now to drop in any other words that you would like to see unfold, any other intentions that you have for your home, your office, your business. See your entire home filling with these energies.

Now you've sent this powerful loving energy into every part of your home, feel that deep connection. While you're in this deep connection with your home, you have open lines of communication. Take this opportunity to ask your home what it wants and needs from you to fulfil these intentions.

Now you have opened the lines of communication between you and your home like never before. It is listening and it is grateful for your attention. Let your home know that you are excited about co-creating with your space and having many beautiful experiences together. Thank your home for listening. Thank your home for this experience.

Take a deep breath in, absorbing whatever you need, then bring your awareness back into the room, into your body, into your breath. Allow yourself a few moments of quiet, while you come back into your space, and know you can drop back into this connection with the soul of your home any time you need to ask your it to co-create with you.

If you'd like to listen to this meditation, you can download the audio version here: https://patricialohan.com/bizmiracles

Your home sees and hears

So, you've cleared the negative energy, you've burnt your negative beliefs away and you've reconnected in the space you live, work and play. Here are three things you can do to begin welcoming in new energy — energy that aligns with your intention — into your home/office.

1. **Clean your front door.** Your door is the mouth of your home that welcomes the energy in. Make sure the handles work, and that there are no cobwebs or dead plants around the door frame. Make it welcoming for new energy. (Honestly, one of my PowerHouse clients lands a new client every time she does this).
2. **Clean the windows of your home/office.** You need to see clearly where your life and business are going. The clearer your office windows, the more clarity you have about what is going on in your business.
3. **Repeat this chapter whenever something negative happens in your space.** The walls can hear so the Sacred Sound Clearing is an excellent way to reset the energy and flush the negativity out of your home/office and business.

SHARLEEN'S STORY:

"I WAS A NEWLY MINTED REAL ESTATE AGENT – NOW I'M NUMBER EIGHT IN MY CITY."

I was a newly minted real estate agent when the pandemic hit, so everything that happened in 2020 pretty much shut down my career. I had been single for a long time too, so I needed something to kickstart life in that area as well.

I did one of Patricia's free challenges and followed through on all the suggestions. After implementing everything she told us to do, like cleaning doors and windows, I noticed a big shift in my house. Then when the PowerHouse programme became available, something told me I just had to do it.

When I got my personalised report from PowerHouse this year, it said my house had gone into a money lock. Last year, I added in the remedies that the report suggested, and the very next day, someone called me to help them sell their house.

In 2021, I became number eight in real estate on Rate My Agent for Mississauga. It's been a transformation for me! Now I'm taking Feng Shui into my real estate business, helping buyers and sellers with what they should be noting, like not painting dark colours in a home because that's a big no-no for energy flow.

Feng Shui hasn't been all about the business for me, though. When I implemented the recommendations in my relationship area, my soulmate appeared within a month! Whether you're into it or not, Feng Shui is a wonderful opportunity to learn new things. It's not just about putting a Buddha statue in front of the front door. There's more to it. It's about making your house into a powerful house, a PowerHouse! It's about changing your dynamic and your thinking. It's amazing how much can shift when you do that.

Chapter Six
MAPPING THE NINE AREAS OF YOUR BUSINESS

Now that you've cleared the space, it's time to invite ease and flow to your business! To do that we are going to learn how to draw a map of either your home or your office space and find the unique energy spots. In traditional Chinese Feng Shui, these are called *guas*, but in PowerHouse, we translate them as Power Centres. We are going to be looking at the size of your home/office and then divide it up into the nine different areas and what they represent in terms of business.

You won't have to make any big structural changes. What we're doing is looking at what your home/office is like and how it's set up. You can choose to do this in different ways depending on your workspace. You could look at your whole home or you could focus on mapping out the nine areas in the room that you use as an office.

The decision is yours and will depend on your circumstances. If you have a designated room, you're free to do that area first, then look at the entire house plan afterwards to identify blocked or cluttered areas. If you don't have a specific office, it's worth looking at the plans for your entire house and working with the areas that align with business, career and money. (My book *Happy Home* goes through the corresponding areas from a personal point of view, which is a nice extension of this work if you want to look at Feng Shui beyond the realm of business. And I highly recommend you do!)

POWERHOUSE PRACTICE: Creating your floor plan

First, decide where you are going to Feng Shui. If it's your home or a commercial space, you are going to need a copy of your floor plan. If it's just your office or desk, you can sketch out a rough shape of the room on a sheet of graph paper with a pencil and a ruler.

If you're drawing your plan by hand, my recommendation is to count out the size of your office with your feet. All you have to do is put one foot in front of the other and count. For ease, I use one square of graph paper per foot, keeping it simple.

No matter which tool you use, try to make sure the outline of your office space is as accurate as you can make it, though don't panic if it's not perfect. It's also important that you can write on your floor plan, so once you have it, make a copy.

What if you don't have the plans for your home or office building? No problem! You can create a floor plan easily with a great free tool called floor planner.com. All you'll need to do is measure your space. Once you have the measurements, enter them all into the tool. It's vital that your plans are to scale and the correct shape. However, you only need the shape and size of your space, not the fixtures, fittings, furniture, or windows.

If you have a home or commercial space with more than one storey, you will only need to make different floor plans if the upstairs is not exactly the same outline as the downstairs.

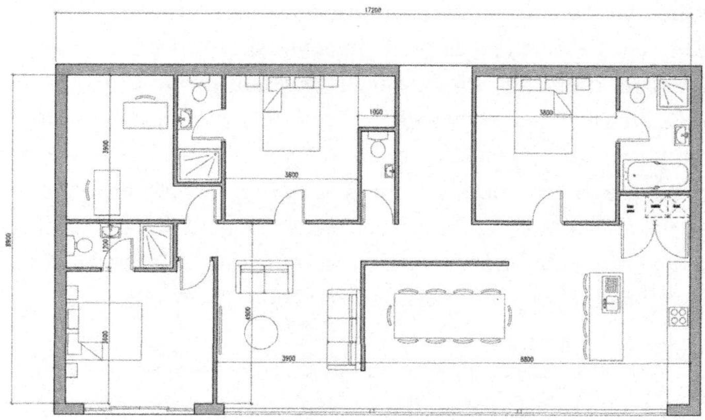

Finding the Power Centres of your business

Once you have completed your floor plan, you'll need to divide it into nine areas by dividing the length into three equal parts and the width into three equal parts as well, like a grid. In other words, measure the length and divide it by three, then measure the width and divide it by three. Draw in the lines across your floor plan. It's important to note that you are looking at the main length and width of the space, ignoring any protruding parts or alcoves. You'll deal with those separately.

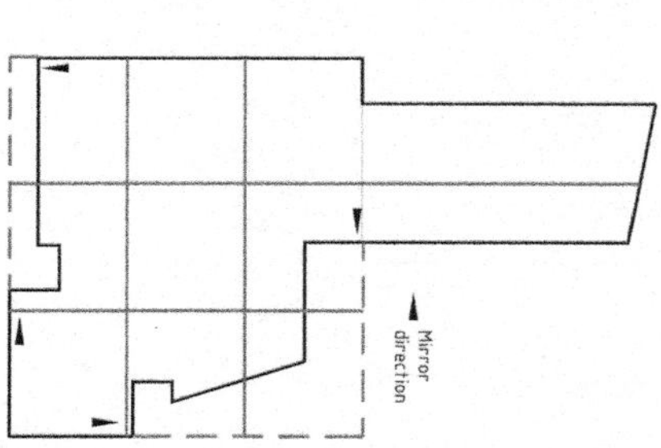

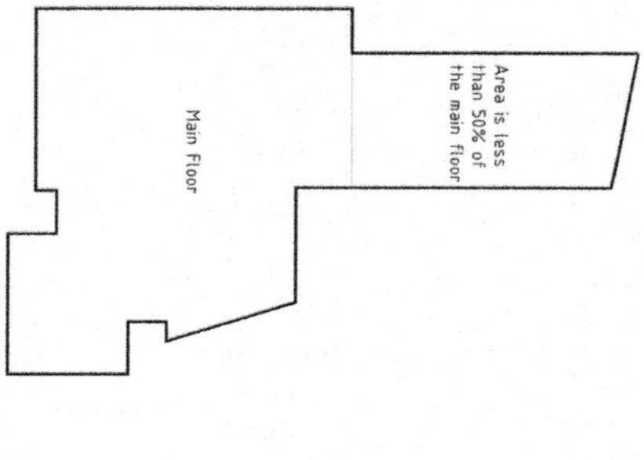

What happens if your space is an uneven shape? This happens all the time! For Feng Shui, the dream shape of any space would be a rectangle. It's great to know this for buying or building property in the future because that makes it easy to Feng Shui. However, it may be the case that you are in an odd-shaped building with bits sticking in or out. This is likely to mean that you will be missing one, or several, Power Centres. When there is a missing Power Centre, the capacity for that space to expand into its fullest potential in that area is lost. This can have serious ramifications for you, your business and your employees.

Here's how we tackle non-rectangular shapes. First, you need to determine whether the area that doesn't fit the rectangle shape is an 'extra bit' or a 'missing bit'. If the length and/or width of the shape or protrusion is less than 50% of the length or width of the floor plan, you can take it to be an extension or an 'extra bit'. This means it becomes part of the Power Centre it is attached to already. However, if the length and/or width of the shape or space is more than 50% of the length or width of the floor plan, it is part of the building's shape. That means you have a missing Power Centre, a partially missing Power Centre or several missing Power Centres.

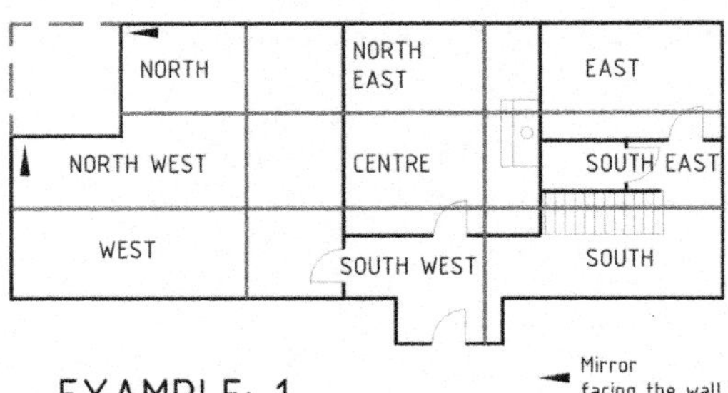

EXAMPLE: 1

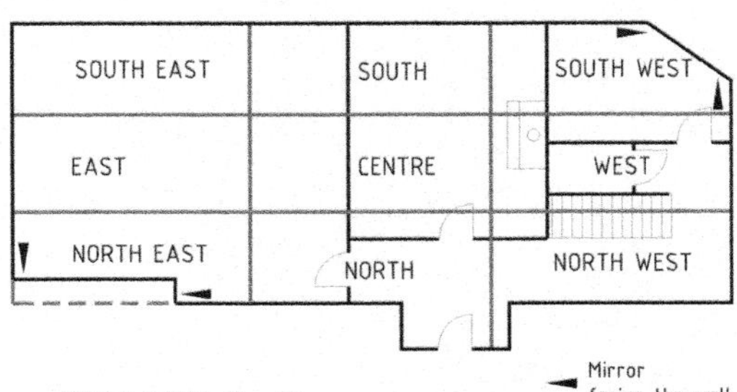

EXAMPLE: 2

Once you have determined where you may have a missing Power Centre, extend the line of your property to create a rectangle. Use a dotted line to signify that it is a missing bit.

Mark the Power Centres on your floor plan for every storey. Each storey might be missing different Power Centres depending on the shape of your house and whether the floors are copies of one another or completely dissimilar.

Ultimately, your floor plan should look like a rectangle, perhaps with extra or missing bits, and with nine equal-sized areas: three Power Centres on the length by three Power Centres on the width; or eight outer Power Centres and a central one.

Compass reading

Now that you have a floor plan marked with a grid of the nine Power Centres, you'll need to know which Power Centre corresponds to which area of the floor plan. This is where the compass directions come in! As I touched on in Chapter Two, Flying Stars Classical Feng Shui relies on the directions of the compass to orientate the Power Centres.

Taking a compass reading is easy! All you need to do is use the built-in compass on your smartphone. You can use a regular compass too if you want.

Here are the steps:

First, find north. It doesn't matter if the compass wobbles around slightly, north is always going to be north. Mark on your plan which of your nine areas is in the north direction.

From there, fill in the rest of the areas: 90 degrees from north is east; 90 degrees from east is south; 90 degrees from south is west. Between those directions, mark on northeast, southeast, southwest and northwest. Use the examples below to help you get your bearings.

EXAMPLE 1:

NW	N	NE
W		E
SW	S	SE

EXAMPLE 2:

SW	W	NW
S		N
SE	E	NE

EXAMPLE 3:

SE	S	SW
E		W
NE	N	NW

EXAMPLE 4:

NE	E	SE
N		S
NW	W	SW

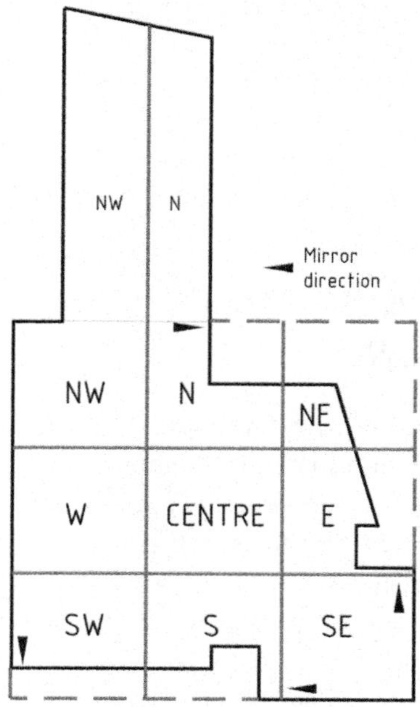

Now that you have your nine-part grid for your home/office and your compass directions, you can assign each Power Centre. Since this book focuses on Feng Shui for business, I've amended the names of each Power Centre. When we do Feng Shui for your home, some of these areas focus on slightly different aspects. If you'd like to know more about Feng Shui for the home and your home life, please check out my book *Happy Home*.

Central:	Health of the business and working environment
North:	Career and business mission
Northeast:	Knowledge and skill-building
East:	Teamwork, growth, new beginnings
Southeast:	Prosperity and power
South:	Fame and reputation
Southwest:	Business partners
West:	Creativity, communication, productivity and marketing
Northwest:	Helpful people and travel

What do you do about missing Power Centres?

This will only be relevant if you're dividing up the areas of your home (or commercial space) rather than just your office space. If you're just focusing on one room, skip this section. For those Feng Shui-ing their whole home, you're going to use mirrors to create the space.

POWERHOUSE PRACTICE: Creating walls

1. Gather some compact mirrors or buy some mirror tiles. The sizes and shapes of the mirrors you use don't matter.
2. Take your floor plan and look at where you have dotted lines. From inside the space, place the shiny reflective side of a mirror facing the nearest wall to your missing Power Centre, projecting outwards towards where you want your wall.
3. The mirror can be hidden and positioned anywhere along the wall, even right at the top of it, or in a corner out of the way. If you don't want it to look too obvious, you can paint the back of the mirror or hide it behind a piece of furniture.

Don't worry if it's not perfect!

Marking out your floor plan and getting it exact is not imperative. As I've said, this book is a beginner's guide to get you started, so you don't have to make this floor plan precise! Just do your best. Realising and having the awareness that you have nine different areas of your home/office space — and that each one represents a different part of your life — will definitely improve the energy alone!

The recommendations I have included in this book are not as precise as the remedies we do in the PowerHouse programme. In PowerHouse, we take all of the information about the home and map out a precise floor plan, giving the exact cures needed in each area. It has a super specific, dramatic effect on the energy in that area!

In this book, what we're doing is intentional rather than specific. You're not doomed if you put a mirror in the wrong place, so don't overthink it! Just do this floor plan as a rough guide and get an idea of where the areas are. Then follow the steps.

With the basic nine areas and directions sorted, you're already beginning to Feng Shui. As always, intention and awareness are the most important part of the process.

CARRIE'S STORY:

"SINCE I'VE FENG SHUI-ED, I'VE HAD MY LARGEST EVER REVENUE MONTH."

I own a marketing agency, which has done well over the years, but I was starting to feel stuck with it. No matter what I did, I just kept hitting a wall. In PowerHouse, Patricia says that it's often your environment holding you back. You can be doing all the right things, but if your environment can't support all of them, you're going to be stuck.

Our house was bad for money, bad for people. I was nervous about putting in all the remedies but it wasn't a big deal in the end. One of my favourite things was writing affirmations for each area of the house. I love redoing them each year to see what I had written the previous year. It feels like completing the process. I think the house is relieved too now it has better energy flowing through it.

It doesn't feel like I'm spinning my wheels any more. My work days feel easier. I don't work as hard. I'm working less and making more money. I'm happier. In the past year since I've had my house Feng Shui-ed, I've landed my largest client ever and had my largest ever revenue month, probably 30% more than I've ever made in any month. I've co-authored a book that went right to the top of the bestseller lists on Amazon, and I bought another marketing agency. My husband unexpectedly got a stock option buyout from the private equity group that invested in the company he works for. It was a lucrative month — and I owe it to Feng Shui!

I'm pretty sure my husband is a full-on believer in Feng Shui now too!

PART 3

FENG SHUI FOR YOUR BUSINESS

CHAPTER SEVEN

THE HEALTH OF THE BUSINESS AND WORKING ENVIRONMENT AREA

This Power Centre is all about cultivating a healthy, nurturing workspace.

Now we've gotten to the fun bit! In each of the chapters in Part 3, we are going to dive into each of the specific Power Centres around your office space, whether you've chosen to do this at a macro (whole house/ building) or micro (room only) level.

Before we begin, a word of caution. There's a lot of misinformation about Feng Shui out there. Every area has bespoke energy and you don't even have to be sitting in that Power Centre for the energy of that Power Centre to be affecting you. If the energy in a particular area is not happy, you are going to see that reflected in your life and business. That's why I suggest focusing on the areas that feel like they'll have the most impact.

The Universe is always conspiring to support and guide us in our next step, so trust your gut on where you are called and add any enhancements intuitively. Sometimes it can feel like what we're doing isn't making a difference, but it will be having an impact, even if that is a subtle effect on the overall health of your business.

So, let's dive in and see what needs to be shifted!

Looking at your floor plan, the central Power Centre represents the health of your business and working environment.

What is currently in that physical space of your home or office? Is it clear of clutter? Does it feel good? Is the energy a bit low?

This space represents your business's healthy bank account, healthy owners, and healthy relationships. Everything that is associated with health and vibrancy in your business will be reflected here. So, it's important that whatever is here represents health, clarity and nurturing. It has to be a good working space for you. Low energy in this area could represent a current decline in the business; whether that's clients, leads, speaking opportunities or anything else.

I had one client whose office was in the centre of her home, and as she opened the door she said to me, "Welcome to the dumping ground!" All this stuff was just cluttered and piled up in the office, and she also reported health problems in the family and the business. Once we cleared the space, things began to change!

One of the problems with the middle Power Centre is it can be limited as to what Feng Shui enhancements you can add. For example, if we were Feng Shui-ing your desk, usually the middle space is taken up by your laptop or keyboard. However, there are a few changes you can make.

ENHANCEMENTS

First things first, you want to keep this space as clean, clear of clutter and as organised as you can. Don't let the clutter build up, because it will impact the health of the business.

If possible, add fresh flowers and plants into this space. Even just a little plant in front of your keyboard in the centre of your desk would do the trick or a laptop screensaver with a field of daffodils! You can be as creative as you like with Feng Shui enhancements, the key is the intention of why you are placing the item there in the first place.

If you have some more space in this area, some good plants that you could add include:

- Areca palm (also known as *Chrysalidocarpus lutescens*) — removes all indoor air toxins, is super easy to care for, and has leaves with a gracious flow that softens the energy.
- Bamboo palm (also known as *Chamaedorea seifrizii*) — removes benzene, trichloroethylene, and formaldehyde from your space, is resistant to insect infestation, and adds a peaceful, tropical feel to any environment.
- Rubber plant (also known as *Ficus robusta*) —removes most pollutants and toxins from any indoor environment, especially formaldehyde, will survive in dim light and tolerate cool temperatures.
- Money tree (also known as *Pachira aquatica*) — is good for enhancing abundance. Plus you can get a small one if space is an issue!

Other enhancements you might consider:

- Place a citrine or amber crystal somewhere in this Power Centre.
- Use either pine or sandalwood essential oil in this area. You could use a diffuser if this is one whole room, or you could choose to spritz something in this area with one part water and three to five drops of essential oil.
- A little statue or picture of Ganesh (remover of obstacles) or Quan Yin (Chinese goddess of compassion).*
- Add to your vision board something that represents your business's health.

*When I mention spiritual deities, these are only relevant if you feel an affinity or if it resonates with you. Feng Shui is not a religious practice. If you read up on the energy of a deity and feel called to use it, by all means do! Please don't feel that you have to use these symbols. Feel free to use a god or goddess that you do personally relate to in that area. It's not a requirement, just an option available to you!

In addition, avoid placing a bin in the centre of your office. If this cannot be avoided, make sure you empty it all the time. This represents clearing out the old energy and inviting in the new.

POWERHOUSE PRACTICE: Writing your business affirmations

Once you've added in any Feng Shui enhancements you like, it's time to set clear intentions for what you want your business to look like. You'll do this for each Power Centre as you work through this book. Here, let's create some affirmations about the health of your business. I love doing this so much as your home and office is listening.

Each affirmations section is an invitation to journal on what is currently relevant to you and your business. There are some examples for you below, but the more specific you are to *you* and *your* business the better. Your office is listening, so put into your own words what a healthy and vibrant business looks like to you.

BUSINESS AFFIRMATIONS:

I am grateful for my healthy, prosperous, growing business.

My business environment nurtures me.

My clients and team support my growth.

My business is healthy and growing.

The Universe provides me with an abundance of amazing clients who want to use my services.

Once you have written out the affirmations that are relevant to the health of your workplace area, place them somewhere in your central Power Centre. You might choose to type them out and have them somewhere you can read them all every day. You might choose just one and have it as the background on your laptop if you are applying Feng Shui to just your desk. You don't have to have your affirmations on display if that doesn't work for you. You could have one word that represents your affirmation as a password or pin them behind a picture or place the written versions underneath a plant pot.

It's completely up to you how you decide to apply the enhancements, and use your affirmations, but what you're doing here is making sure that your environment knows what you want in your business loud and clear.

PATRICIA'S INSIGHTS:

I had one client who used to be a chef and had retrained as a Tony Robbins coach. When I was in her office, all I saw were cookery books on her shelves. "But you're a Tony Robbins coach," I said. "Where are all your Tony Robbins books? Your personal development books? Where are the things that represent what you want to do in your business?"

That's an important question for you to answer too. Where are the things that you want to represent for your career or business? Are they in your office or workspace?

The client moved her cookery books to her kitchen and rededicated her office to her work. Twenty-four hours later she rang me to say she'd been inundated with requests from new clients. It was an overnight transformation.

The health of our careers, and our lives in general, is all down to the alignment of our thoughts, beliefs, actions and environment. The thoughts and beliefs that come up are the internal work you have to do.

When it comes to your environment, Feng Shui balances the energy and brings your office into alignment. Just like your body's homeostasis,

Feng Shui moves your home into a state of balance. When your home is tapped into alignment and flow, everything else starts to flow. Even if things are okay, small tweaks and changes can improve the health of our businesses, ourselves, our jobs, whatever we're doing.

POWERHOUSE PAUSE

Check in with the health of your business here and identify what you can implement asap.

What can you do right now to help the health of your business?

What is that one small step you could implement?

How can you track the state of your business health?

What's going on every month?

What have you done?

What has improved?

What hasn't improved?

Look at the numbers and get comfortable with analysing your business. This is the only way you can know your business's health. If you don't know the health of your business, understanding what needs to happen next will be far more difficult and you'll waste time taking actions that are not in alignment with your goals. If you feel some resistance here, that's natural, but it's such a powerful step when you tune in and take action.

LAUREN'S STORY:

"I WAS AT BREAKING POINT... FENG SHUI SAVED ME."

Last year, in August, everything was going wrong. I had just moved into my dream home, right next to the beach, all brand new with a swimming pool. It was so beautiful and expansive! It was a dream situation. Until it wasn't.

The day I moved in, two of my major private clients cancelled on me. I'm a positive person, so I made it mean that they weren't in my highest alignment.

What I didn't realise — until I joined PowerHouse — was that the house I had moved into, this beautiful dream home, was bad for money in Feng Shui terms. Literally the day I moved in, money stopped coming into my business. Compared to normal, I was barely breaking even on my finances.

I help people attain financial freedom in small easy investments, so I had my own savings and it wasn't a big deal at first to lose those two clients. However, I only brought in one or two clients from the time I moved there in August until January the following year.

I tried to get things started, but nothing was working. I couldn't get moving in that area at all. I was exhausted and completely burnt-out. I had zero passion for what I was doing, zero energy to think up any other ideas. I was at breaking point. I was even losing friends. It was crazy what was happening in this house, my brand new dream home!

Thankfully, I was lucky enough to have my house Feng Shui-ed with the PowerHouse programme. I only did it because I thought Feng Shui would be kind of nice, but thank God I did, because then I learnt about the areas I needed to work on!

Within a couple of weeks of implementing the specific recommendations for my home, I received a tax refund, which had been outstanding for around five years.

The other major area that needed work was community. Since I implemented all the remedies Patricia gave me, I'm happy to report I have lots and lots of friends again!

I'll be completely honest, my level of burnout before I went into PowerHouse was just so, so tired. Everything felt heavy. PowerHouse felt like the last possible thing that could save me. Yet once I made those changes, the brain fog started to shift. That was the biggest thing I needed. Now, I couldn't be more excited about the future.

Chapter Eight

THE CAREER AND BUSINESS MISSION AREA OF YOUR BUSINESS

This Power Centre focuses on your reception area and first impressions, communications, and your ability to express yourself through your business.

Let's talk about the north area of your home/office. This north area represents the career and business mission. It's also where I would recommend you set up your reception if you have a bigger office space. Your reception area is the first impression of the business. This Power Centre is also about communications and the ability to express yourself through your business.

POWERHOUSE PAUSE

Are you a good representative of your business? This is food for thought for this Power Centre. You can journal about this to create your business affirmations for this area. This Power Centre invites you to look at your business mission. Take a moment now to think about that. Why are you here? Why do you do what you do? What do you want to do and how do you want to support people? Who do you serve? Be specific with who it is that you want to help create a better life.

Here are some other questions that can help you get clarity on your business mission:

1. What price do you charge? Why?
2. What are your guidelines for selecting who you support?
3. What are the boundaries you have around your business?
4. What is the first impression you want people to have around your business?
5. For online businesses, how do people feel when they land on your website? For in-person businesses, how do they feel when they enter your space?
6. How do *you* feel when you land on your website? Do your spirits rise or fall when clients arrive?

Once you are specific about your business mission, you can clear up certain elements of your business to bring your first impression into alignment. That includes making sure your logo and website align with the mission and vision, the colours you use reflect it, and even the clothes you wear. The more aligned all of these little elements are, the clearer and louder your message becomes.

Make sure what you're putting out there into the world has a super positive first impression that aligns with where you want the business to go. Here's an example. Let's say you sell wellbeing products, but your website homepage is dark and dingy or your office lighting makes you look pale and drawn on camera. That's the kind of first impression that could be off-putting, since it reflects illness or low energy. As best you can, walk your talk.

Having a strong, powerful statement will help you move forward with your business, attract your dream clients with that clarity and repel what you don't want. If you already have a mission statement, make sure it's still relevant. Your business might have changed and pivoted since you first wrote it, like mine did before I reconnected with Feng Shui, so it's worth looking at again. I recommend revisiting your business mission at least once a year as your business goes from strength to strength. If you have never written one or you need a rewrite, go and do that now, stick it on your wall, and be clear what you want your business to stand for.

POWERHOUSE PRACTICE: Give your business mission statement a boost

Download yourself a copy of the business mission statement in my companion journaling guide from ***www.patricialohan.com/bizmiracles***

Complete the following phrases to get you started:

I help ...

I only work with ...

I absolutely reject ...

Without my help these people will ...

This makes their life a living hell because ...

But with my help they will ...

The way I help them get results is ...

In exchange for helping my clients get these amazing results, my fee is ...

The number of clients a month I will work with is ...

I do my work because ...

POWERHOUSE PRACTICE: Start a business vision board

To accompany your business mission statement, you might want to begin creating your company vision board where the mission statement is included, along with the logo, colours and any other visuals that represent your business mission and vision.

I love to divide my vision board into nine areas and put something in each Power Centre. Add images as you go through the other Power Centres in this book.

Remember your home/office is listening as you do this work! Back in Chapter Five, I talked about the windows seeing and the walls hearing everything that happens in your space. The foundations you lay for a balanced and harmonious home/office will allow your vision board to come to life.

ENHANCEMENTS

- Create your business mission statement as per the exercise above.
- Write down your underlying drive in your business. What is your desire? Why are you on this mission? Find a mantra, buy a piece of art, or print out a list that aligns with your mission. Keep it in your career and business mission area, so that your energy is reinvigorated every time you look at it.
- Sit with your team (if you have one) and see if they can clearly articulate your business mission. If they can't, put together a

workshop session so you can all get clear on it together. Your team represents you and your business, so they need to know this!

- Do the same thing with your clients. Create a questionnaire or survey to see what their first impressions of your business were and if they can accurately guess your business mission. If they can't, tweak your communication to new clients and make sure it aligns.
- Check your advertising, your promotions, your website, to make sure there is one clear mission and vision that you present to the outside world.

Here are a few quick, fun Feng Shui tweaks you can put in place:

- Place a piece of black obsidian crystal or black tourmaline somewhere in this Power Centre.
- Use bergamot, pine, rosewood or spruce essential oils in a diffuser in this room, or spritz something in the area these essential oils diluted in water.
- Have a small statue or picture of Tara (Hindu goddess of wisdom) or Athena (Greek goddess of wisdom) somewhere in this Power Centre.
- Place your affirmations in this area.

BUSINESS AFFIRMATIONS:

Just like in the last chapter, here are some affirmations for this Power Centre. Use these alongside your business mission statement. You want to make sure you choose affirmations that clearly reflect your business mission so that your business is fully integrated. These are simply examples. Using your own affirmations will always be more powerful if you are clear on what you want. Take these suggestions and merge them with your own intentions. This is the best way to call in what you want.

I have a clear business mission that supports myself, my family and the greater good.

I have clarity and excitement about my fulfilling business as I am passionate about helping others live the life they deserve while earning abundance while doing so.

I have excellent relationships with everyone who works for and with me.

I attract all the right clients, and employees for an abundant, fulfilling, rewarding and successful business.

I am confident, earning a wonderful living doing work and service that is important to me, using my skills and talents which I am grateful for.

I am grateful that I am attracting the perfect opportunities and circumstances to have the business that I love and that is financially rewarding.

I trust that the opportunities for success are coming to me and my business in a balanced and harmonious manner, for my highest good and the highest good of all concerned. And for this, I am truly grateful.

PATRICIA'S INSIGHTS:

"I help..." is probably one of the most important statements you'll ever make for your business.

I help people get... peace.

I help people get... clarity.

I help people... do their accounts, secure a mortgage.

What you're doing in the world is so important. It's having such an impact on people's lives and this has a ripple effect! When we focus on how we are serving, it changes everything. We become more magnetic to more clients, more abundance, more money, more attention in the media *because* we are coming from this place of selflessness. In my experience, when you tap into your heart, your business starts to take off!

My *I help...* statement is this:

I help women raise the energy in their homes so that they can tap into their divine wisdom, flow, abundance, ease and joy. This allows them to be happier, flourish and shine, it allows their partners to be happier (or for them to call in a partner), and it allows their kids to be happier.

As part of crafting your business mission, my final pro tip would be to dig a little bit deeper. Ask yourself *why* are you *really* doing this? Yes, businesses have to make money but you could make money any way! Why *this* business? Be honest with yourself. What are you doing to help change people's lives? What is the ripple effect of that?

Focusing on the positive attracts more positivity into your world. If you're struggling with this, try meditating to align your energy with your intention before you do the business mission statement exercise. This is a great way to clear your mind. Daily meditation before you begin your work day is one of the best things you can do to align your mission and energy.

If you're still stuck, ask your current clients how you can serve them better in their everyday lives. What are they looking for? Focus on ways to make their journey better and easier. Show up for them more than you think you need to. You might think you're pestering, but clients are busy people! They'll take all the help they can get. The more you keep talking to your customers and the more you listen to their problems, the easier it will become to gain clarity on exactly how you can help them. Think about the negative impact of them *not* working with you too. What will they stay stuck in?

Just don't try to be everything to everyone! Pick one thing. I was the Mary Poppins of healing modalities. I had learnt all of the tools and they were useful for my skillset, but if I'd offered my clients all of those treatments at once, it would have been super confusing. When I narrowed my offering down to just Feng Shui and then used my full skillset within my PowerHouse programme, I started to see real traction in my business and clients results.

The clearer we are about who we serve, what our mission is and the impact we have, the easier business gets. Without a clear path of what we want to achieve and who we want to help it can be impossible to keep any momentum going. Your business mission should pull you forward, rather than making you push and trudge through every day. It can even be the reason you get out of bed every morning.

JOJO'S STORY:

"NOTHING WAS HAPPENING, AND THEN MY DREAM JOB JUST APPEARED IN FRONT OF ME."

I was looking to buy a new home and it was stretching me financially. I needed a bit of reassurance, and one of my friends was doing the PowerHouse course, so I joined.

I created an Excel spreadsheet of what each room does and where I needed to put the remedies. Then I created a vision board and a list of what I actually wanted. My number one dream sat in my career section; I wanted to manifest more money. When Patricia asked me to dig deeper, I realised it was about wanting to be in a job where I felt appreciated. I wanted to earn a certain amount of money per year, sure, but I also wanted work-life balance and a company car.

I put that affirmation in my career corner and left a note there with the remedies. I wouldn't allow anybody else to touch it. Patricia told me to think about the remedies first. Everything else was a 'nice-to-have'. I went deeper into the PowerHouse programme. That's when I knew it would come.

One of the other things on my vision board was travel. I wanted to travel the world without worrying. So, I went on holiday to Thailand, and was enjoying being present, when an email came through from work. It said there was an opportunity to pay me redundancy. At first, I thought, "That doesn't go with my goal of wanting a promotion and pay rise" but I had this feeling that I needed to take the redundancy package, irrespective of whether I knew what the outcome looked like. This went against my vision, but I said to myself, "Right, okay, trust the process."

My redundancy came through. By April of the same year, my dream job just appeared in front of me as I scrolled the job pages. It met the salary expectations I wanted and came with a company car. The company prioritised work-life balance and I could work from home. It was everything I had written on that piece of paper. I applied for the job and received an offer in July.

I almost tripled my salary with that job. The salary I had written on my vision board would have taken me over 1,000 years to attain in my old role!

One last goal was left on my vision board: I wanted passive income. I had no idea what this passive income would be, but I knew I wanted it, so I could have more holidays and another security blanket. I decided I would invest my redundancy money in a card manufacturing business. I have somebody else working for me in that business who runs the whole thing and I make some money on the side, which has potential to grow.

My husband was a complete cynic when I started my Feng Shui journey. He went from 'this doesn't work' to asking me to write him an affirmation. His business has gone from being a two-man band to employing teams of people. For anyone wanting to do Feng Shui, you don't need your partner on board. Remedies can still work even if they're not interested!

CHAPTER NINE

THE KNOWLEDGE AND SKILL-BUILDING AREA OF YOUR BUSINESS

This Power Centre is all about training and development, resources to grow and improve, your business library and computer networks, and your team's ability to be open-minded to learning and trying new things.

This is the northeast Power Centre of your office space, which represents knowledge, self-cultivation, wisdom, intuition and meditation. As someone who trained in lots of healing modalities, I truly believe that trusting your intuition and using meditation can take your business forward in leaps and bounds.

This is your spiritual and educational area. Now, if you have picked up this book, you probably don't believe your business is *just* a business. It's what you've been called here to do. It's your mission. You put your heart and soul into it. As well as encompassing personal development and team training, this Power Centre is also where you tap into that divine force that helps drive you to share your light and be of service in the world.

For this area, you need to be clear on what you want to learn next in your business and what growth you want to experience. That means taking a look at your business mission statement and breaking down your bigger picture into steps you can implement. What's the next step to take? Perhaps it is learning a new social media platform. Perhaps it is getting your first piece of PR exposure. Could it be hiring a new team member or updating your website? What skills do you need to cultivate in order to achieve that next step? Remember, Feng Shui is all about intention.

POWERHOUSE PRACTICE: Your next skill

Journal on the next skills you or your team need to develop in your business. Write out exactly what is needed to achieve this. Ask yourself and your team members:

What are you curious about?

What would you like to learn?

How does it relate to the business?

How much of a priority is building this skill when you look at your business goals?

This area is also about your spiritual connection and activating your intuition. You know what's best for your business, but you also have to be open to taking on other wisdom.

When I spent time listening to the soul of my business, what I heard was like an angry teenager. My business told me, "Just let me go and do what I want to do! Stop trying to control me! I know what I'm doing. I'm growing up now!"

POWERHOUSE PRACTICE: Listening in to what your business wants

When you tune in, you'll notice your business has wisdom all of its own. All you have to do is sit down and have a little chat with it! Take your business out on a date and journal about what it needs. Ask your business:

How are you doing?

What do you need?

Where do you want to go?

Free write and let your business respond to you. This is a great way to tune into the personality of your business and connect with the essence of what it wants. Give it a try and see what personality and essence of your business comes through. Ask for higher guidance and let your business have a say in where you can both serve best.

Remember, this is the Power Centre of resources, so look at what you already have, what you need, what may need updating, and what no longer serves you in your business. As your business grows and you hone your craft, resources that you used as you were starting out may no longer be relevant. Think about what moves the needle. It's always worth checking in on what you're paying for that you don't even use or doesn't bring results.

Take stock of your software and tech systems to see what needs updating. If you have a team, they will likely be able to give you clear feedback on what they love to use and what they don't, so ask them! Having the right tech systems in place saves you both time and money by automating many of the laborious tasks. And you will keep your team happier if you harness the power of the internet and cloud-based software to make their job easier. The happier they are, the more willing they will be to try new things.

As your skills, intuition and resources develop over time, the intention of this Power Centre may change more often. This process, as my PowerHouse clients have mentioned, is never-ending. It is a practice. And the more you incorporate it, the better results you will yield.

Here are some 'set and forget' Feng Shui enhancements you can make to this area to get started.

ENHANCEMENTS

- If there is a particular platform or tech you want to improve your skills on, print out the logo of the company and place it in this corner or on your vision board.
- Place any personal development, self-help or business books you want to read in this area. If you have enough space, you could choose to make this area a library or set up a bookshelf.
- You might choose to add to this area of the room or your vision board pictures or quotes from people in business who inspire you.
- Add a small statue or picture of an owl, Athena (Greek goddess of wisdom) or Saraswati (Hindu goddess of knowledge) to symbolise wisdom and knowledge in this area.
- Make this your meditation space to connect to your intuition. If you can't meditate here, you may choose to put crystals such as green jade or green fluorite in this area instead.
- Diffuse or spritz lemon, peppermint or rosemary essential oils in this area.
- If you're considering a career change or would like to acquire knowledge in a new area, keep related books, study materials, and degree prospectuses here.

BUSINESS AFFIRMATIONS:

Below are the business affirmations to use in this area. As always, feel free to tweak any of them to suit you and your business. If you have a team, this is a great chance to sit down together and have a brainstorming session! Team members will have their own personal development needs. Involving them is a great way to play to their strengths and skills. Their growth will only help your business grow too!

I am intuitive and I trust my intuition.

I am listening to my intuitive self.

I follow my own intuition in my business to take the right steps

I always listen to my intuition before I make a decision.

I trust my intuition with a deep sense of security.

I follow my intuition where it leads and I always find gifts that evolve my soul.

I am connected to my own inner vision.

I see possibilities and bring them into my reality.

I am clear. I am connected to my true path and purpose.

I am true to myself. I am completely in tune with the presence of the Divine within me.

I trust my intuition and follow Spirit without hesitation.

I see myself constantly learning, which is easy and enjoyable. And for this, I am truly grateful.

I see myself continually growing in greater self-awareness and expanding my consciousness. And for this, I am truly grateful.

I have an abundance of time and capacity to learn.

I expand in all the ways I choose.

I am mastering new skills that bring me confidence, fulfilment and joy.

Every day, I realise new abilities and talents.

I have time, space and the finances to feed my mind with new ideas and understanding.

Everything I read brings me new and wonderful insights.

PATRICIA'S INSIGHTS:

One of the things I wish I'd known when I first started my business was that you are your biggest asset. Investing in yourself and your skills is a vital part of your business growth and success. There's no such thing as a wasted investment when it comes to you.

Of course, that doesn't mean you have to *do* it all yourself. Many entrepreneurs get trapped in the cycle of doing it all themselves in the beginning. I know I did! For ages, I tried to do it all on my own. I would wing it all the time. Now my advice would be that you don't have to jump between all the courses and learn it all yourself. Instead, have a clear plan on what it is you need to learn next to move your business mission forward. Then decide who the best person to learn from is. Get that course and train in it. If you can't train in it, then ask yourself who you can hire to support you in this area of your business.

Don't do what you're not good at.

You will grow as your business grows, but not everything is *vital* to get perfect right now. Don't complain when things go wrong. Just assess. What happened? What went well? What didn't? Did the results surpass expectations or fall short? What contributed to that?

Learning is a part of doing business and I'm still learning. You are going to get it wrong sometimes. You will learn more from those times than the times you get it right. Complaining that you don't know why something is not working or why you're not getting the results even though you did *all the things* isn't going to make your business start performing! Be honest (but kind!) with yourself about where you could improve.

If there's something that you hate doing, be brave and bold enough to invest in someone else with that skillset to give you a hand. Whether that's a business mentor to check your blind spots or a VA for a couple of days a week to do your admin, the more support you have, the more likely you are to succeed. More money in the hands of the people you hire is better for everyone too.

Avoid falling into the trap of having to have the best and most expensive things to succeed! If I could give you any advice, it would be to do what is *easiest* and most suits your budget, especially if you are building an online platform or programme.

Nowadays I have high-quality videos with great lighting, but this wasn't always the case. When I started, I used to use a slideshow. I had a screen-share recording as my content, because the thought of being camera-facing was totally unachievable for me at the time. It's a journey to get comfortable teaching on camera, so don't feel like it has to be polished and perfect from the get-go. Learn and tweak as you go.

Going with the best of the best isn't always the smartest move either. For one Feng Shui programme I ran, I built an entire bespoke dashboard with a beautiful aesthetic and it cost a fortune! Then it couldn't handle the sheer numbers of members we had and kept crashing. I had to pay an assistant to reset people's passwords all day. When I switched back to a cheaper hosted teaching platform, it worked much better and cost us less too.

Try new things as you stretch outside of your comfort zone. You'll find your business and the tools you use will grow with you naturally. It's important to realise you don't have to do everything perfectly in the beginning. Keep it simple, stick to the process, and put your offers out there.

GRETA'S STORY:

"I STEPPED INTO KNOWLEDGE THAT WAS ALWAYS INSIDE ME. I'D NEVER PAINTED BEFORE, BUT NOW PEOPLE ASK TO BUY MY ART!"

I'm an occupational therapist and artist, but despite this, I knew I wasn't spending enough time on self-care or living my life to its full potential. I had kids and a business. There was a lot to juggle. The truth is, though, I hadn't given myself a clear direction for my goals.

Before PowerHouse, I had tried everything. I had been to healers, psychics and business groups. I used to run away to the US every single year to recharge. I had this nagging feeling in my bones that something wasn't quite right.

I jumped into PowerHouse with a group of my business friends and decided to share the ride and experience together. The reason I chose to do it was because I'd already chatted a lot with Patricia at an event and she was warm, friendly, energetic, and most importantly, she was real and authentic.

What I got in PowerHouse was clarity, in my life, in my house, in my goals. I put my faith in the process and set clear intentions. And it worked! Within the timeframe I'd set, I'd found my house *and* been offered work unexpectedly.

The real shock came when I started painting. I had never painted before. It was just something I knew was inside me. I only wanted to do it for self-care, but now I have people asking me if they can purchase my work and telling me I could have an exhibition.

When all these results started happening, it made me realise the power of Feng Shui and setting clear intentions. I got exactly what I asked for when I became clear on my business, my life as a mum, and my self-care routines. The house I bought ticked all my boxes and the monthly income figure I wanted was the exact figure people were offering me.

Since doing PowerHouse, I have stepped into a knowledge that was always there, but that I didn't fully believe until I saw it for myself. My life no longer feels like a circus. It feels much calmer than it was before. Feng Shui shows you why that is and it is astounding to understand what is beneath the surface.

CHAPTER TEN

THE TEAMWORK, GROWTH AND NEW BEGINNINGS AREA OF YOUR BUSINESS

This Power Centre is all about business structure, leadership, new projects, past and present supporters.

The east section of your floor plan relates to your team and extends to your community. Think about the organisations you and your business belong to, directories you are in, charities you support and any online or in-person communities where you build your network. In essence, this Power Centre is all about the people you surround yourself with.

Let's start with your business structure and who does what in your team. You want to be playing to everyone's strengths and cultivating the dream team. Get your team to set and share the intention of the business together. If you want to set your business affirmations yourself, that's no problem, but encouraging your team to use those intentions as mantras when they come up against a problem or for a mindset shift is a great way to make sure you are all growing the business in the right way together. This helps set the positive energy of the team and customers and potential clients will feel this as they engage with your business.

If you don't have a team yet, write out which team members you will eventually need, including their ideal traits and personality, as well as their job description. I have done this every time and it has worked like a dream. Hiring the right people is vital. You want team members who are trustworthy, kind and motivated. And ideally, people who love their job! The clearer you are, the easier it will be to manifest the right person for your business.

Now that you're clear on your intention and your business mission, take a look at the organisations and communities you engage with professionally. Do they line up with your mission? Do they hold the same values as you? You want to make sure you are aligned with the right people who can help propel your business forward.

If you donate a percentage of your profits to charity or would like to go on to support a charity through your business, what would it be and why?

POWERHOUSE PAUSE

Who do you align with? Spend some time journaling and getting clear on who you want to be surrounded by and who you in turn would like to support.

Write out a list of the organisations, communities, networking events you'd like to attend and any charities you would like to support. Look into each one to make sure it aligns with your business mission, values and goals. Then start brainstorming ways you can collaborate with these people.

ENHANCEMENTS

This area of your office space is an ideal spot to place a photo of your team all together. You could have just one singular image or a collage of all your team days together. Maybe you could have a spotlight selfie of each team member doing something they love. Anything that shows you care about your team members. If you don't have a team, you might add a picture of a team that you aspire to having.

You could also have photos of the charities you support or logos of the businesses and organisations you work with in this area or on your vision board. Symbols of a group of people holding hands can work well here too.

Other enhancements include:

- Having a small statue or picture of Hera (Greek goddess of family)
- Keeping rose quartz or aventurine crystals in this area
- Using pine or sandalwood essential oils in either a diffuser or spritz.

BUSINESS AFFIRMATIONS:

This is the perfect place to also put a business affirmation that you and your team work on together. Below are a few ideas to help get you started.

I am blessed with a beautiful, well-balanced, enthusiastic aligned team.

I nurture and am nurtured by wonderful family and friends, teammates and colleagues, with love and kindness, patience and goodwill.

I have a happy extended like-minded community filled with health, respect and love.

My team and community is motivated, healthy, happy, safe and full of love!

I am a source of love and inspiration for everyone around me as they are for me.

My team, family and friends are a beautiful reflection of the Divine's love.

I am excited and delighted that I'm blessed with happy, harmonious, healthy relationships in my life and business.

I am delighted to be experiencing greater harmony, ease, flow and joy in all areas of my life in a balanced and harmonious manner for my highest good.

I am grateful for my talented, productive, passionate team of like-minded souls. I feel supported, connected and loved.

PATRICIA'S INSIGHTS:

This area is also about those who have supported you *so far* in your business, and those who support you *outside* of your business. Your friends and family may have helped you get started, or perhaps an old business colleague introduced you to a current client.

Take a moment to write a gratitude list of all those past and present supporters and reflect on how they have supported your business so far. Practising gratitude for what you already have goes a long way in helping your business go from strength to strength, rather than always wondering when more is going to arrive. It's something that changed the way I felt about my business when I was just starting out.

Don't be shy to ask for testimonials. Ask all the time! Find out more about the results people get from working with you, what support they felt they received, what they loved about working with you, and what they may have liked even *more.* Understand what has gone on to happen in their lives since working with you, even if they don't work with you anymore. Not only can you use these answers and insights on your website, in your sales copy, or in your book, but their results will also give you a clear idea of the A to B journey your ideal customer experiences when they work with you. You can then emphasise those results and points when talking in your communities to your prospective customers and future buyers.

You should always be looking to foster new connections, so get out there and socialise with people! If you don't like networking in person or if you're more introverted, make sure a more extroverted and chatty member of your team goes out and about speaking to people about the business, telling people how easy it is to work with you.

Again, the easier you make this, the more people will come. People want a clear step-by-step way of how to work with you. The fewer steps, the more likely they are to start. Take a look at your website, your social media pages, and anywhere your business is featured. Is it clear to see what offers you have and how people can get them? Are all your sales pages easily signposted? Is your pricing clear? If you have enrolment dates for a course, is this clearly explained on your website? Get fresh pairs of eyes to give you feedback so you can make your impact even clearer as your business grows.

Plan for your growth! When you need support, which team members will you need first? For six or seven years, every day except Christmas, I used to answer everyone's questions in our PowerHouse Facebook group. Now we train people in our PowerHouse Feng Shui certification and have hired some of them so they can help me answer questions and it allows us to offer 24/7 customer service. How quickly their questions get answered is one of our members' favourite things! I also have people who have been in the community so long that they answer the questions too. Answering every question myself was a burden, but once I decided I didn't have to be the person who addressed the Facebook group, that was amazing.

What are you holding onto that someone else could be doing? What is suffocating you? If you're the one trying to hold it all together, you are likely sabotaging your next big leap in business. For me, I couldn't handle the volume of people we were bringing into our launches. I was the bottleneck, because it was a question of how I would cope with a million questions! Now that we have dedicated people supporting me to answer questions in the group and the best bit is they answer exactly how I would have, I feel comfortable having launches where hundreds of people join at a time.

MEL'S STORY:

"MY CONNECTION WITH MY TEAM HAS SHIFTED COMPLETELY."

Over 20 years ago, I experienced a miscarriage. It was a spiritual transformation for me. It changed the focus of my life. Within a year, I had left my corporate role and trained to be an acupuncturist to help heal people.

I did every healing course I could and mastered several healing modalities in two years. Then clients started coming to me wanting to fall pregnant and the healing worked. I started mentoring women in the Law of Attraction and they started getting pregnant too. With that success, I wondered how I could help women with other problems in the same way.

Suddenly, they started to turn up, asking me to help them with all sorts of other issues, from problems with family members, exes and attracting narcissistic relationships, to debt and money issues. As my practice was always full, other practitioners kept asking me questions about how I achieved this, so I started to mentor other practitioners on attracting clients. Now they have full practices too.

It was overwhelming for a time and I was struggling to concentrate. Doing the PowerHouse course was a complete transformation for me. My office is in my house and the basics of just shifting the space around were unbelievable. It became a completely different environment.

Now I am so productive. I find it easy to concentrate and no longer feel overwhelmed, which has resulted in me helping more people and making more money than I have ever done before. It's been fantastic.

More than that, though, it's a perception thing. Patricia talked about trying to move forward in certain ways and the energy of your home bringing you back to its vibration. As a healer, I know everything is energy, but it didn't click that, of course, your home is energy too. Having a vibrationally supportive base was a game-changer for me.

Feng Shui has shifted my abilities so much higher, and my connection with my guardian angels and all my team has transformed.

As an acupuncturist, I knew about the five elements and I had wanted to employ a Feng Shui consultant for a long time, but I tried to muddle through on my own. I should have known better. I now believe that you attract your home as the perfect match to your energy when you buy it. If you want to make changes in your home, you need to raise the energy of it through Feng Shui, so that you can attract higher vibration people, money, situations and longed-for babies into your life.

Once your home is constantly vibrating on a higher frequency thanks to the Feng Shui placements, any internal energetic work such as releasing energetic imprints, low vibe thoughts, feelings and beliefs will become easier to do. The Law of Attraction will result in creating a life of your dreams.

It's been incredibly powerful and I recommend that everybody do Feng Shui. Especially if you're feeling stuck and you feel like you're going one step forward and two back, Feng Shui is the place to start.

Chapter Eleven

THE PROSPERITY AND POWER AREA OF YOUR BUSINESS

This Power Centre is all about an abundance of business, clients, cash flow, profits and opportunities.

In this southeast area, we are going to focus on your business goals for yourself. It is just so important to take a step back and get clear about what your financial goals are for your business and how much you want to earn. This is the wealth, prosperity and abundance area of your business after all!

So, what do you want in abundance? First, take stock, because it's easy to attract abundance of what you *don't* want if you aren't super clear. Worrying about bills? Guess what. You may attract *more* of that by putting all your attention on it.

POWERHOUSE PAUSE

Take a moment now to journal on wealth, prosperity and abundance in some detail. Below are some questions that can help you:

What does abundance mean to you?

How much do you want to make in your business?

What are your financial goals?

What do you consider prosperity or prosperous to mean in terms of your business?

What do you want your business to look like?

What does prosperity feel like to you?

What would it be like to have the most prosperous version of your business?

POWERHOUSE PRACTICE: Look at the numbers

Reflect back on the business mission statement you did in the earlier chapter. Going through that document will give you a clear path of where you are and where you want to go. You can set financial milestones alongside that. Perhaps you just want two clients a week. Maybe you want 50 clients a week. Perhaps you are clear that you want to earn $500 a week. Maybe that number is $50,000.

Using the clarity from your business mission statement, determine how you are going to bring those numbers of clients into your business and at what prices.

All you have to do is the maths.

Journal on what you want an abundance of in your business and start anchoring in how this abundance is going to come to you. You can come back to this exercise time and time again! Your business will ebb and flow constantly like the tide. What you want in one business quarter you may have plenty of in the next, so your priorities will shift.

Alongside your internal clarity, you will want to make sure that your external environment looks prosperous. This Power Centre should *feel* abundant. That doesn't mean super expensive — but anything in here does need to feel positive and uplifting.

ENHANCEMENTS

Here are some Feng Shui tips that might give you that 'oomph' you are looking for in this area.

- Place a little bowl with money overflowing into that area. If you want to amplify your prosperity even more, have the bowl sitting on a mirror or mirror tile. This represents your money overflowing and is a great visual anchor to remind you there is always more money.
- Place amethyst or citrine crystals in this Power Centre.
- Use an essential oil diffuser or spritz bergamot or frankincense.
- Write a cheque from the Universe for the amount of money you want to make this year and place it in the money bowl. (You can download one from our special bonus sections here ***www.patricialohan.com/bizmiracles***
- Write the number from the cheque on your vision board.
- Place a money tree or lucky bamboo in this area.
- Have a spiritual statue or image of Lakshmi (the Hindu goddess of wealth and good fortune) or Fortuna (the Greek goddess of abundance and fortune).

If you're feeling scarcity around your business, or you just feel like there's not enough coming in right now, it's important that your home, office and this Power Centre, in particular, feels abundant. You want to walk in and feel amazing.

Start with the enhancements above, then take stock. Look for items that are broken or depleted and get rid of them, because these will be impacting your business's prosperity. If you bring in plants, make sure they are upward-growing.

Over time, you might decide to set aside some of your business budget to upgrade things in this area of your office that don't feel as abundant, prosperous and luxurious as they could. Make a list now of each of the items in this area and rank them according to this scale:

1. First class — It's perfect. The most abundant, natural, organic product that you wouldn't change for the world.
2. Business class — It's good and does the job, but you would have liked to get something a little better.
3. Economy class — It was all you could grab at the time, it's broken or doesn't work properly.

Work through the economy class items one by one until, eventually, everything reflects the abundance of your business. Yes, IKEA furniture might be great to get you started, but is that the long-term vibe you want to hold? As you start improving the energy and vibrancy of your goods, it improves the energy of your office, home and business, and spills out into your clients. Start by making sure these items are first class when you can: a great chair, a good table/desk and a great laptop. We'll be going into more detail about these things in Part 4 of this book.

POWERHOUSE PRACTICE:
Taking stock of your abundance

Create your first class, business and economy class list. Tackle the broken or depleted economy items first. Here's a few ideas to get you started.

ITEMS	FIRST	BUSINESS	ECONOMY
Desk			
Chair			
Laptop			
Filing cabinets/storage			
Books/bookshelves			
Communication/email systems			
Artwork			
Notebooks/pens/ stationery			

BUSINESS AFFIRMATIONS:

Finally, it's time to add your affirmations to this area. As with all the affirmations, use the below ideas as a guideline to create your own. You are more than welcome to use these, but the more personalised they are to you and your business, the more effective they will be.

Think about a statement that will make you *feel* the most abundant and prosperous first. Then use the clarity from your earlier journaling on what prosperity in business means to you to create something super specific. Print it out and put it somewhere only you can see it, or save it as a reminder on your phone for when you start your business day. However you choose to use your affirmations, it doesn't matter. What's important is the intention you set, so that you can align with that abundant feeling whenever you see the reminder.

I am constantly in the energy of abundance on every level learning and improving in business, which is easy and enjoyable. And for this, I am truly grateful.

I have an abundance of time and money to do all the training I require and can expand in all the ways I choose.

Abundance is my birthright and flows to me easily.

I am rewarded with immense abundance as a result of fulfilling my life's purpose.

Every day in every way I am getting better and better, I am realising new abilities and talents which benefit me and my business now.

I have an amazing relationship with money

Money comes to me in increasing quantities from multiple sources everyday

I love money, money loves me.

My capacity to receive increases every day.

I am blessed with an amazing team in my business that I can easily afford.

I have a happy bank account and money flows to me easily through my work.

I am a trust fund baby of the universe.

I accept that which I choose to experience in my life, which is a happy, harmonious, healthy relationship within my family. And for this, I am truly grateful.

I know that I am experiencing greater health and wealth in all areas of my life in a balanced and harmonious manner for my highest good. And for this, I am truly grateful.

PATRICIA'S INSIGHTS:

Money comes with a lot of emotions and I've gone through many evolutions of my personal relationship with money. Ultimately, my advice in this area is to watch your thoughts around money and how you spend it. Whatever you are saying to yourself you are manifesting and putting out into the world, and your house is certainly listening too! It's time for you to become friends with money, to look at your numbers and to become grateful for what you have.

For the longest time, I used to shy away from money. I was afraid to look at the numbers or go to meetings about my finances. It was all just stories in my head. When I worked for my family business, we were always afraid of meetings because it was always bad news. When working together, Ken and I decided to flip that on its head and have meetings to *celebrate* how money came into our business. The results were amazing and we felt so much more grateful for the money coming in!

One way you can get on board with gratitude around money is seeing everything as an investment. Those bills you pay? Look at what it gets you! A roof over your head, warmth in your home, food in your belly. Those taxes you pay? They're a sign that you successfully made a profit this year! Celebrate!

This attitude goes for selling too. Your client's money isn't 'gone' when they pay you. It's an exchange of energy. When they come into your programme or get your services, they're gaining that programme or services. They are investing in their future.

A lot of the fear around money in business is about sales. Understand that selling is *helping*. Selling is being of service! You have something that other people want or need and are willing to pay for. It's your job to get out of your own way and tell them about how you can help.

Remember the impact you desire to create with your business mission. It's super important to keep reminding yourself of that 'I help' statement you made. Helping other people is the biggest part of what you've come here to do, so hold that reminder strong when you are selling, pitching or launching. Trust that taking inspired action will mean the right people who need your work will show up in your world.

There are always women who are shocked when I tell them they should be emailing their audience regularly and selling regularly. They think it's too much. But it's not too much. It takes as much as fifteen touch points before a typical client is convinced, through seeing enough of your content, emails, social media posts and testimonials, that they want to come and work with you.

What happens when that one email gets lost in their Spam or Other email folder ? What about when the social media algorithm didn't show your post to them that day? You think you're selling and talking about your stuff constantly, but just a small fraction of your audience is seeing it. And they need to see it a lot more to want to buy and benefit from how you can help them!

Of course, you will have dream clients that come in and want to work with you straight away. We love those! Do you know what convinces them? It's often not your client testimonials or your sales page copy. Usually, it's your energy! People buy from *people*. If your energy radiates worth, value and love, that's what clients know to expect when they are in your orbit.

This is where your money mindset comes in. You might be looking at the figure you wrote down at the beginning of this chapter and thinking, "I'm not worth *that* much money! What I do isn't good enough to charge *that*!"

Here's the thing. Your thoughts affect your reality. If those are your beliefs, that's what you're going to be projecting out onto clients. Working on your money mindset is as fundamental as selling every day. You have to work on the limiting beliefs that say you aren't good enough, or worthy enough, or loveable enough, and tell yourself a new story about money that you can get behind. Surround yourself with the affirmations and items that make you feel that way every day, and you'll soon start to see your mind telling you a new story.

Of course, not everyone in business helps their clients to make money. So, what do you do when your result for your client is 'you'll feel healthier' or 'your home will have a nicer energy'? When I was starting out, helping people deal with their anxiety, trauma and stress, I didn't have a tangible number to put against that. That's probably why my business struggled in the beginning. When my business pivoted to Feng Shui, people could *see* my results. They could *see* that I'd built a business that allowed me to travel with the world as I worked. They could *see* that I was becoming more and more successful. They could *see* that I'd manifested the love of my life. And so many women want that! My clients wanted these same goals. And when they asked me how I did it, I said "Feng Shui." You can do this too. Become the role model your prospective clients need. Embody those results that you provide your clients.

Look at how you have created results so far. I bet there are things in your life right now that you longed to have just a few years ago. Think back to how you achieved that. What did you do? What did you think? What did you believe? How much money did you spend getting to that result? What were you willing to pay at each stage of your journey? Plot your answers into your ideal customer journey alongside your business mission statement. Eventually, you'll be able to recognise what your skills, experience, expertise and offering to the world is worth.

When your prices change

As your business grows, you're going to start seeing some interesting changes. For our Feng Shui programme, we have incrementally increased the price over a number of years. When we did that, we noticed something amazing. The higher the price of our programme, the better the results our clients would get.

One day, we opened the doors for a new round at the course's highest ever price point and something felt weird. We'd raised our prices before and it had gone well. This time, we were making as much money but seeing fewer clients. It was like we'd hit a volume threshold. I meditated on it and we changed the price back and gave everyone who had paid the higher price a VIP hour with one of our PowerHouse Feng Shui consultants. After that, the numbers of people in our membership returned to that expected level again.

What lesson can you take from this? You must tune in with *what is right for you*. Step out of the launch or the business for a moment, get away from it all and the right thing for business will come through to you.

Over time, you'll start to see the value of your offering and feel more comfortable telling people about what you are doing. That could be a package, a programme, a service. It could include content, group calls, 1:1 time, or a mastermind. There's no right or wrong way on how you deliver it. It just has to work for you and your client.

Remember, your ideal client is someone who has a high priority to solve a problem or get a result. It's highly important to them. It's not a 'nice-to-have'. It's something they *know* they need. They're at a specific point in their journey where they're perfectly positioned for you to be the next person they hire.

Your price point isn't about the number of months or sessions or modules they have with you. It's about how they feel at point A and what value they will have by the time they reach point B. You don't have to do tonnes of 1:1 time with them, and you aren't responsible for their results. These will be money beliefs for you to work through. They don't have to buy something cheaper from you first, although some clients will, and there are people in your audience right now who are your ideal client! They just don't know it yet.

You have to explain to them how your A to B journey is unique. There's an expert for everything, right? The clients who hire you don't just do it because you can help them get these results but because of who you are. Your personality, your experience, the modalities that you've developed. These are the differentiators that will make you prosperous and abundant in business!

RITA'S STORY:

"MY DAUGHTER GOT OFFERED A JOB AS A SOLICITOR IN TWO DAYS."

I'm an interior designer and I came across Patricia and her PowerHouse programme when I was moving to a new house. It was the crappiest-looking house on the block, but I didn't mind because I could see the potential it had.

When I moved in, though, I started hitting problems. I had this brand new wood-burning stove and the glass shattered down the front! I could feel this strange force and I thought the house was spooked. I needed to find out what was going on with this house, so I worked through everything in PowerHouse.

My daughter's bedroom is in the prosperity area of our house, and even though she didn't care about the Feng Shui, she respected what I was doing. She kept her room tidy and didn't seem to mind when I put the specific recommended cures in there. Then, on her second day back to her job after her holiday, she was offered a job as a solicitor. She had only just passed her exams when she was given this opportunity at the place where she had been working as a paralegal. That's a big win for me because that's all you want as a parent —to see your children happy and successful.

Of course, I've had success as well. I tagged a company in a post about this gorgeous wallpaper and they sent me two rolls and all the paint I needed for a job, which was a £400 win.

Now I've gotten the house to a good place, I'm doing Patricia's vision to reality. I'm re-evaluating the direction of my business, because even though I have my own house and my own business, I want to ensure everything continues to flow. Doing PowerHouse, I feel a lot more comfortable and confident going forward.

Chapter Twelve

THE FAME AND REPUTATION AREA OF YOUR BUSINESS

This Power Centre is all about public relations, branding, awards, and future goals.

The south Power Centre of your home/office that we are looking at in this chapter represents fame and reputation.

POWERHOUSE PAUSE

Get your pen and paper out and start journaling about this. Dig as deep as you can. Think about what you want them to say when they refer you to someone else when they write you a testimonial or when they introduce you at events. Think about the tone you want to be spoken to on the phone, in person, and over email. What you want reviews about your business to say. Get clear on what you want you and your business to be known for.

The questions I want you to answer here are:

How do you want to shine your light in the world?

What do you want to be known for?

How do you want people to talk about you and your business?

What do you want your reputation to be?

What does fame mean to you?

How does it feel to be well-known for what you do?

Awards and accolades fit into the picture in this Power Centre. When Stephen Spielberg hired a Feng Shui consultant to work on his home, she found his two Oscars on her way to the toilet. The consultant moved them into Spielberg's office and placed them in his fame and reputation area. She also made him order another lookalike statue to sit alongside his other two as a representation and intention of manifesting a third Oscar.

What awards or accolades would you like to win for your work or your business? What things have you already won or had press over? What media outlets do you want to be featured in?

This Power Centre is all about how you shine your light in the world. Where is that? Is it on TV? Is it in a particular magazine or newspaper? Is it being featured on a blog? What podcasts do you like to listen to? Where do you like to spend your time and be visible? What platforms might you have already been featured on?

Get even more specific and dig into which social media channels you'd like to have an impact on. How many followers do you have on Facebook, Instagram, YouTube, TikTok? Which platform do you most enjoy spending time on? Which platform has bought you the most clients so far? Where do you have the best engagement?

What would it mean to you or your business to be famous? Play that scene out in your mind and let your imagination run wild, taking note of how much money that brings in, which people come to mind straight away, and what your audience size across email and social media looks like. Add these to your business vision board.

Then think out and write the practical steps it would take to achieve these things, however wild you may have dreamed! Could you go ahead and hire a PR company? Would you need to write a couple of articles to pitch to your dream media source? Might you start building a relationship with the partnerships you want — engaging with their emails or their social media accounts? You can write these answers into your business mission plan once you're clear on these too.

Before you skip this section and think it's not for you, I want to acknowledge that you may not want to be super famous. This Power Centre is more about how you want your business to be known. Maybe you are happy behind the scenes. Affirm exactly what you want for your business and how you want it to play out when you come to writing your affirmations for this area.

ENHANCEMENTS

When it comes to your office, take some time to look around and identify potential partnerships. Perhaps there's a certain magazine that you keep in your reception or a radio station that you and your team always listen to. Your environment is already mirroring back where you subconsciously want to go in your fame and reputation area, so start hunting!

Other things you can do include:

- Placing a citrine or coral crystal in this Power Centre.
- Using an essential oil diffuser or a spritz of bergamot or frankincense.
- Placing your diplomas, certificates or awards clearly in this area for all to see.
- Putting an award or recognition you'd like to win on your vision board.
- Having a small statue or image of Brigid (Irish goddess of the sun) or Apollo (Greek god of the sun) somewhere in this Power Centre.

BUSINESS AFFIRMATIONS:

To get behind the belief that you and your business can truly shine a light in the world and make a huge difference, here are some business affirmations you might like to incorporate, tweak and place somewhere in your fame and reputation Power Centre.

I am so grateful that I have been interviewed by XYZ on their show.

I'm so grateful that I have attracted incredible, pure publicity for my business in XYZ magazine.

I'm so grateful that my business has been featured on XYZ podcast.

I am respected, admired and appreciated for the work that I do.

My clients and I have wonderful relationships. And for this, I am truly grateful.

I am recognised for my skills, talents, and accomplishments. And for this, I am truly grateful.

I share my light, gifts, talents and passion with the world and earn an abundant living doing so.

Whatever your intentions for your business, affirmations are there to help you get your message clear and distinct. If someone was to look at it, they should be able to tell it's about you and your business. You must be able to link your message with your business mission too.

Affirmations are also there to help get your message shared widely. When you're writing them, consider how you want your message to be shared.

PATRICIA'S INSIGHTS:

For years, one of the things on my vision board was writing a book. When it happened, it was an amazing accomplishment! The first book I wrote was also great for the reputation of my business. In the three years since I wrote it, I've been in The New York Times, on TV and so much more. I remember a good friend of mine saying, "Write a book because it's a brilliant business card!" Turns out, she was right.

When I was in America, people would automatically say to me, "Oh *you* wrote that book." When I appeared on TV, they would mention that I have a book. Writing a book gives you authority in your area of expertise. I even got paid to be on TV as a Feng Shui expert. When I published my book, it was like the world took a bit more notice of me.

If you're scared about reaching out to media outlets, don't be! They're looking for stories, especially if you're working in your local area. There's always a local newspaper that needs content. I used to do a load of charity fundraising, so I would call them up and say, "I'm doing a quiz for such and such charity." A journalist would always turn up, take a photo and write a little something. Then local people started saying, "Oh that's Patricia Lohan." Don't underestimate the power of local business! It's just about getting yourself out there and being seen.

Talk to journalists like a normal person. They are human beings. Ask them where to go to get featured for your product or service. If you don't get any help, move on to the next paper. Aim your talk at those who are looking for help. The rest doesn't matter.

If you're feeling that imposter syndrome, go back through your client testimonials and success stories to remind yourself of what a great product or service you have.

With my book, I knew what I wanted to share. My talking points were clear to me, so my message was clear to the audience. The book was amazing for credibility too. It was just how I wanted to boost my reputation. Yours might not be a book. It may be the same or it may be something else. It depends on what you're comfortable with and where you're at with your business.

Think about where the book or media exposure can take you. That's what the fame and reputation section is about. What can you use as a launchpad to get your business in front of people? What do you want to be known for? And how can you best showcase that expertise?

Getting media, PR attention, awards, acknowledgements and accolades is easy when you are clear on what your message is and how your expertise can help.

Remember to dream big, like I told you at the beginning! What would be the wildest, craziest, most amazing outcome that could happen from this exposure? What would it look and feel like? Many of my clients have achieved incredible results when they started to focus on where they were going. You can have this too!

ANNEMARIES STORY:

"YOU HAVE TO BE CAREFUL WHAT YOU WISH FOR BECAUSE YOU JUST MIGHT WIN BUSINESSWOMAN OF THE YEAR."

When I started Patricia's PowerHouse course three years ago, my husband and I had moved into our West Cork farmhouse that was over 200 years old. The office of the house wasn't great. I'd gone through and cleared out a lot of stuff during the move, but we were still stuck. Money was coming in, but it was going out as fast as we made it.

Feeling so stuck was driving everyone down, and impacting our relationship, our kids, everything. It felt like a constant battle.

At the time, I had just started my business and I had very few clients. I knew nothing about Feng Shui whatsoever, but I went into the programme wanting support for my business, for John's farm, for people to show up and help us.

My husband is a typical Irish dairy farmer and thought it was all woo woo. At that time, he told me, "AnneMarie, this won't work." But my business was a pressure cooker and I needed something to change.

I did all the little things I could. I'd go into one of my Power Centre areas, tweak this or that, wipe away the cobwebs and clean the windows. Then one day, my husband came in and said, "AnneMarie, the money is just flowing in!" So, I thanked the house.

After that, all sorts came in: hotel upgrades, prizes for local draws. I even won €2,000 on the lottery. Throughout it all, I kept making the small changes that Patricia recommended in PowerHouse, one at a time, layer by layer.

That's when it happened...

I had said I'd like to be featured on one of the biggest TV shows here in Ireland... and the house must have been listening! I've now been featured on TV, in national papers, in interviews on the radio and in articles. Plus, I've won the national Businesswoman of the Year Award in my area.

When you start a business, you have to work with everyone and anyone, but I now have a two-month waitlist of ideal clients. Every time I do some Feng Shui, I'll get an interview request or something. It just goes crazy! You have to be careful what you wish for because you might just get it!

The changes, evolution and growth are mind-blowing with Feng Shui. I always tell people to go for it, because they will not regret it. Feng Shui rocks. It changed our life. If you're like me and you are sometimes afraid to talk about what you wish for because it might come true, then know that it is a constant process.

CHAPTER THIRTEEN
THE BUSINESS PARTNERS AREA OF YOUR BUSINESS

This Power Centre is all about suppliers,
contracts and human resources.

The business partners Power Centre is the southwest area of your office space. In PowerHouse, when we are focusing on people's homes, this Power Centre represents love and relationships. In a business sense, though, it actually represents business relationships, including suppliers, contractors, and even human resources. If you have a big office space, this would be the best position for your HR team to sit.

If there has been trouble with suppliers, contractors, or staff, this is the area that you want to look at, because this Power Centre concerns the connections that you have in your business. If this is something you need ASAP, start by decluttering and getting a clear and defined affirmation up in this Power Centre!

If there's no trouble, but you want to attract the *right* connections, use that as the intention for this chapter as you Feng Shui this area. It's the perfect way to create amazing partnerships.

ENHANCEMENTS

Because this area represents partnerships, we want enhancements that are going to accelerate that.

- If you have images or artwork in this area or on your vision board, look for pictures of you and your business partners, clients, or suppliers together. If you don't have these, even a corkboard with your logo and the logos of all the people your business works with would do the trick. You can even add images of those people you want to work with in the future.
- Using images is a powerful way to use the intention of Feng Shui, so you might also consider putting up a picture of your team here, if you didn't put one in your teamwork area for whatever reason.
- If this isn't the ideal space to put images, you could just have a folder in that area where all this information is on your team, business partners, contractors and suppliers. Keep the folder green for nurturing growth, red to attract the right ones in, or purple to manifest them. Keep your affirmations for this area in the folder too.
- Write a list of your dream partners, suppliers, contractors and clients. Put down their exact avatar, the full description of who they are, what they want, how old they are... etc. Then, alongside that, add an affirmation like, 'I easily attract these people into my business.'
- Include black obsidian or black tourmaline crystals in this area.
- Use jasmine, lavender, sandalwood or rose essential oils in either a diffuser or spritz.
- Statues or images of Quan Yin (goddess of compassion), Aphrodite (Greek goddess of love), Cupid or angels also work well here.

Most importantly, try to keep *everything in pairs* in this area, even the artwork and crystals. You don't want any lone images or solitary objects, as these represent being alone. We're not going out of our way to make huge changes in this one. It's about thinking about pairs, groups and good connections. You want a group feel, that sense of buzz and vibrancy you get from people who interact well and bounce off each other. Even images of people shaking hands would work beautifully! That's the type of feeling we're going for in this space.

We cover more considerations for partnerships in the helpful people and travel chapter coming up, but for now, remember that anyone you're communicating with can be influenced by this Power Centre. I invite you to get clearer on the types of partnerships you want and anchor that into your office space or home, along with the enhancements that you feel called to use for your business and life.

BUSINESS AFFIRMATIONS:

I am grateful for the incredible business partnerships I have.

I am attracted to the perfect partnerships in my business.

I am grateful for the increasing number of clients that I attract easily into my business.

I am a client magnet!!!

New clients flow freely and easily to me.

I enjoy meeting new clients and being well paid for the work I do.

The Universe provides me with an abundance of amazing clients who want to use my services and can easily afford me.

My business is healthy and growing.

It's okay for me to be prosperous and for my business to grow.

I am so grateful for this synergistic relationship, the perfect partners, and for calling in my ideal client every day, all the time.

I expand in abundance, success and love every day as I inspire those around me to do the same.

PATRICIA'S INSIGHTS:

Back when I was teaching yoga for €5 a day on a Tuesday lunchtime, I remember seeing Denise Duffield-Thomas online. I'd known her since I was 19 and I saw her promoting this online course. I bought it and I've now been a member of that community for over eight years.

In that course, I learnt how important community was. Until I was in it, I didn't realise that it was *people* who spurred you on, not the information. It's the momentum of seeing other people having successes that helps you to think bigger for your own life and take action. When you don't know what to do starting out, there's nothing better than having people around you who can answer your questions, recommend books, or help you set up your systems. When people focus on how they can help you, and then you pass that on by focusing on how *you* can help people with what they need, that's when your network starts to light up with opportunities!

That's why I built community into my PowerHouse Feng Shui programme. Now the supportive Facebook community is one of things that members comment on how supportive and useful it has been.

The help you can provide in a community comes back to that 'I help…' statement we talked about in the beginning and the ripple effect your work has on the world. It's one of the biggest things I have seen in my business. The more my team and I focus on supporting our community, getting their questions answered, helping them with other programmes, the easier it has been for my business to grow.

TARA'S STORY:

"THEY JUST FLOCK HERE! IT WAS MY FIRST MILLION-DOLLAR YEAR."

Patricia and I were at an event for business owners and we got chatting. I was buying a new house and Patricia had mentioned something about helping your house work with you. She told me you should clear out anything that may be working against you without your knowledge.

I teach other business owners how to organise their email marketing and write powerful emails. I was in the second year of that business, my husband was already a stay-at-home dad, I was pregnant again and we were in the process of selling the first house and buying the next. I didn't know how any of it was going to work, but I knew I was going to need some magic! So, I joined PowerHouse.

When I got my house plan with all the remedies, I was gung-ho and excited. I took responsibility for doing all the work and found it so much fun. We put such intention into the house and how we wanted it to support us!

One of our big goals for the house was that we wanted it to attract people. Our previous house had always felt kind of cramped and awkward to accommodate people. This time, we wanted our house to be the most welcoming space for all of our friends. Our highest value is to spend time with our friends.

Even when we were placing intentions around our house, we would say, "This house is a magnet for the most amazing people." Now every Friday night, we have a gang that comes over. They bring food and delicious meals. It's just an incredible space for people. They flock here!

One of the other things we did was setting up my office to support me because I work from home most of the time. I loved what Feng Shui and the programme did for my family, but also for my business, because now my office is a sacred space. I feel so supported in this office. I love coming here. I'm just as excited to go back to my desk as I am to start the weekend and hang out with my family.

My business continues to grow at the fastest rate I am personally able to hold. It supports us year after year.

When I first came to Patricia in my second year in business, I was thrilled with what I earned, but I was also like... what else? I was in an early stage of my business and I didn't know what I was trying to do other than just make tonnes of money. Now, even organising my personal remedies, writing my intentions and putting them in different areas of my house each year is such a powerful exercise.

Often, I think I don't want to do something. It's so much work! Then I do it and the results are incredible! Looking back is powerful because I can see how much I've grown and how my goals have changed. Maybe I don't want that goal anymore. And if I wanted it, I got it.

Chapter Fourteen

THE CREATIVITY, COMMUNICATION, PRODUCTIVITY AND MARKETING OF YOUR BUSINESS

This Power Centre is all about your ability to problem-solve, get along, and project completion.

In your home, the west Power Centre represents creativity, children, fertility and new beginnings. When it comes to your business that translates into creativity, communication, productivity and marketing. Like childhood development, this is all about how your business develops.

Much of what you *do* has probably already been covered in the other Power Centres we've worked on so far, and in your business mission statement and vision board that you've been cultivating as we work through this book. Now it's time to hone in on how you want your business to *develop*.

POWERHOUSE PAUSE

There are many aspects to this area, so you must ensure that you tune in to the ones you wish to enhance the most. Reflect on that now:

What do you want to create?

How do you want to express yourself in business?

What would move the needle in your business mission?

What do you want the world to know about you and your business?

Creativity

This Power Centre is about letting your childlike nature and light out to play in the world. There are so many 'rules' when it comes to business, but the only thing I've found to be true is: your business journey will be unique to you! So, harness the creative potential of you and your team by using this space to think outside the box. If your office is large enough, perhaps you have a games area like Google and Apple do for their employees. Even something simple like adult colouring books can help calm a team member and tune out their 'thinking mind' long enough that a new idea presents itself.

POWERHOUSE PRACTICE: Make an inspo list!

Make a list of productive creative outlets and figure out which ones work best. Write a list of your favourite things to do and get your team to do this too.

When you're feeling burnt-out or the creative juices aren't flowing, step away from your business for a moment and do one of these things. Work your way through the list and make note of any activities that renew your sense of creativity.

It could even be as simple as a walk in nature. If that's the case, placing a vibrant image of nature in this area of your office will do wonders to boost your creative energy.

Communication and productivity

Any good leader knows that their team is the heart of the business. If the team is not happy, everything in your business suffers! Good leaders make time to support the needs of their team. Making staff a priority fills up their cups, so then they can go and do their jobs to grow the business.

If you have a large office space, where each team member has their own desk, you can set them up in their best personal directions. I'll share more about that when we get to Part 4 in the power element chapter. If you don't have a large office space, not to worry. Maybe you use this Power Centre as an area where staff can bat ideas around. You might put a suggestions box here or something that can spark their creativity. Perhaps it's even a self-care spot.

Inviting good practices for everyone and creating space for that helps the energy in the team to flow. Remember, no one can pour from an empty cup! Encourage productive lunches; like a walk in the local park, a gym break and/or access to a meditation room. Offer talks on healthy eating, productivity or mental health. This will help raise awareness of self-care and help your employees develop better, which means your business will develop better too!

ENHANCEMENTS:

Other little, easy enhancements to include in this area are:

- Placing a piece of citrine or carnelian crystal.
- Using an essential oil diffuser or spritz of either lavender, rosewood or chamomile in this area.

- Having a spiritual statue or image of Saraswati (Hindu goddess of creativity) or Lakshmi (Hindu goddess of wealth and good fortune).
- Including your branding colours on your business vision board.

BUSINESS AFFIRMATIONS:

And of course, having a business affirmation in this Power Centre (either one of your own or one of the examples below) will enhance your intention in the space too.

I welcome new beginnings in my business and trust in the divine process of life.

I see myself easily expressing my creativity in many ways in my business.

I am productive and organised in my business.

All of my staff are efficient, organised and productive.

All of my marketing is effective and has excellent results in attracting my ideal clients into my business.

PATRICIA'S INSIGHTS:

When you're getting started in business or if you hit a plateau in your existing business that you can't seem to move past, it can be hard to know what to do next.

As well as the Feng Shui changes you choose to make, this wonderful practice from one of my mastermind friends, Prema, is a favourite of mine.

POWERHOUSE PRACTICE: Self-coaching

Take out one blue pen and one red pen. In blue, write out any limitations or fears you are having about your business. Put down any blocks that are coming up, any frustrations, any overwhelm. Free write in an uncensored, unfiltered way.

When you're done, put down the blue pen and take a pause to connect with your higher self, your wisdom, and your heart.

With the red pen, coach yourself on exactly what the right next step is. What do you need to know right now? What do you most need to communicate right now? What wants to come through you right now?

POWERHOUSE PAUSE

If the issue is getting prospective clients to reach out to you in the first place, go back to the self-coaching exercise and ask yourself what would feel like the *best* possible way to get a client.

Would you like to have more business through referral?

Would you like them to reply to one of your email campaigns?

Would they send you a Facebook DM?

Would you like to host a masterclass or co-host one with someone you know well who already has a following?

Would you like someone to read your vulnerable share on your about page and email you directly?

Spend a bit of time envisioning how you would like clients to come and an idea will present itself to you. Then you'll know what to do.

The better you get at self-coaching, the more capable you will be at guiding your clients and any prospective clients too. You know when you jump on a sales call with them and they come with all these blocks or fears or limitations? The more you practice this skill, the better you get at coaching and creative problem-solving.

MARIA'S STORY:
"IT'S LIKE SOMEBODY PLUCKED A PEBBLE OUT OF THE PIPE THAT WAS BLOCKING THE FLOW, AND NOW IT'S GUSHING!"

I'm a manifesting mentor who works with entrepreneurial women, teaching them how to create their life on purpose by tapping into the power of their unconscious minds. I blend the Law of Attraction with everyday practical strategies so clients can have more money, time and joy — the easy way.

After I met Patricia, I realised my home needed to be in vibrational alignment too. I was teaching people how to get into vibrational alignment in themselves, so doing PowerHouse for my environment made perfect sense.

At home, my children were a little uneasy. Business was good but felt like hard work. And I was secretly blaming my husband for things being harder than I knew they needed to be.

I went all out for PowerHouse. I did every single thing Patricia told me to do. I got all the remedies and put them in straight away. And my husband was super supportive, so it was epic! The shifts have been incredible! I'm sensitive to energy shifts, so I could feel everything as we put in the remedies. At first, I thought, "That's nice. If that's all I get out of the programme, I'm happy."

Then my husband's finance business — that I had stepped out of a year before to focus on my own thing — went crazy! He had the busiest period he'd had in two or three years. He's done it all on his own, but everything just flowed.

Through the growth period, he found some amazing backup support people who are just fantastic. And that was after having our main support person go on maternity leave and wondering what we were going to do.

My own business doubled after I put all the Feng Shui remedies in place, and then it tripled the following month.

What's more, I feel calmer and more in flow. My family is much more relaxed after we implemented the changes and our family life is harmonious. It's like somebody plucked a pebble out of the pipe that was blocking the flow, and now it's just gushing!

CHAPTER FIFTEEN

THE HELPFUL PEOPLE AND TRAVEL AREA OF YOUR BUSINESS

This Power Centre is all about business networking, client, customer and vendor relations, legal protection, mentors, and the ability to take your business to 'new places'.

Helpful people and travel is the northwest Power Centre on your home or office floor plan, but what does that mean for your business and how your business supports you? This is about having more connections and connecting to the right kind of people. That can mean clients, but also having successful teamwork with customer-vendor relations and other support people.

It's also about legal protection, making sure you are protected in all aspects of your business, knowing what support you need, who can help and what aspects they can manage so you can grow your business. Maybe you don't need any of that at the moment, but this chapter invites you to look at what it could look like later down the line.

Other helpful people could be mentors and any staff you need to bring you to the next level of business. For example, perhaps you want to be seen on a global or a national platform and need the right team members to support you with that. Maybe you need to be intentional about who you are calling into your business.

POWERHOUSE PAUSE

You know what's coming next... Dream big! Think about these questions and answer them in your journal.

What do you want in your business?

Who do you need in your business?

What could a mentor do for you?

How would they support you?

Go ahead and journal on all the ways you could be supported in your life, and have some fun thinking of out of the box ideas!

Also consider asking for help from Spirit. Feng Shui is such a practical tangible modality, but we have to always remember that there are energetic helpers too. Whether you call them angels, guides, Wisdom, God or the Universe, you can ask for help from those entities too.

POWERHOUSE PRACTICE: Write a to-do list for the Universe

I love to write a big to-do list and then just hand it over to the Universe and say, "Can you look after some of these things for me?"

Give it a try!

I used to be one of those people who tried to do everything for my business. Slowly and surely, I learnt the tool of outsourcing and that is what this whole area is about. What do you not have to do yourself?

POWERHOUSE PRACTICE: Future job descriptions

Write a list of things in your business that you need support with or don't like doing that somebody else can do for you. For me, it was video editing and scheduling emails at first. And I don't do my accounts, they drive me crazy! I found people who are excellent at and super excited about video editing, organising emails and putting my accounts together for me.

This may seem far off right now and you may be thinking you don't need support because you can do everything yourself. You might not be able to afford support yet. Whatever your situation, I encourage you to do this exercise anyway. Identifying the roles you will eventually need in your business will help you call in those helpful people when the time is right.

When you write out the job descriptions of all the people you would hire if money was no object, it encourages you to think about what it would be like to take your business further and have more impact. It's about having the capacity to grow beyond what is right now. Get specific with what help you're looking for in this list, even if you're only starting small with a virtual assistant for an hour or two a week.

The attention to detail is important here. Write out exactly what people will be doing in these jobs. It will be so powerful and transformational for your business.

As you do this, I want you to notice what happens to your shoulders when you start to unburden all of that responsibility onto the page. See what feelings come up for you in your body when all the tasks you don't want to do are handed over and you have more time to focus on the things you love, like working with your clients. *This* is the energy you are going to introduce into this area now.

You can never invest too soon. Even basic support in your business will help you learn to delegate, work better with others and have more time to do the important work.

Think about things outside of your business that you could delegate too. In your home, could you outsource something that would take the burden off you so that you could focus more time on your business? When Ken and I began outsourcing in our lives, we got a cleaner for our house. That was a huge weight off my shoulders because we had a large house and the floors were white! I found it so hard to work while constantly thinking, "Oh I have so many jobs to do and the bathrooms to clean." I didn't have time to do the work I needed to do *and* clean the bathrooms.

The cleaner was happy because we employed her and I was happy because I had more time and space for everything that needed to be done in the business. It also meant I had more time to call in more abundance, clients and money.

ENHANCEMENTS

Some other Feng Shui tweaks you can make in this area are:

- Add a globe or a picture of the world to represent where you want your business to go.
- Put on your vision board a picture of a country where you want to expand. Be clear on where you want to be seen and what places you want to go.
- If you put up a map in this Power Centre, pinpoint the places where your product or clients come from.

- Keep any business journals in this area where you brainstorm about taking your brand regional, national or international.
- Place clear quartz or turquoise crystals in this area.
- Use an essential oil spritz or diffuser in this area with either lavender, peppermint or pine.
- Keep a little statue or picture of Ganesh (remover of obstacles) in this Power Centre.
- Put those job descriptions you wrote into a purple folder to help with manifestation, a red folder to attract those people now, or a green folder if the descriptions are for things you want your team to become as it grows.

Your business needs a sense of direction. These suggested changes are designed to show the energy where you would like the business to go. Sometimes literally. One client I worked with asked her team, "Where do you want to go next?" And they all roared, "London!" That was the next place they wanted to set up an office, so we put up a picture of London and the company logo in the helpful people and travel Power Centre. I also had them write affirmations to accelerate this process.

Go back and reflect on those journal questions in the beginning of this chapter. What would it mean for you and business to have support? What can you create when you have more support?

BUSINESS AFFIRMATIONS:

Once you have given the journal questions some thought, merge those answers with one or several of the business affirmation examples below, or write your own, to bring clarity on the direction your business is moving.

I am grateful for an abundance of people to help me whenever the need arises and to support me and my business in the perfect way.

I have an abundance of supportive people in my business who allow it to expand and prosper.

I trust that the right people come to me at the right time to help me in my business so that it grows and expands with ease and joy.

My business supports me to gracefully travel as I choose, and live the life of my dreams while running a business that I love.

My business is recognised globally!

I have the time and the unlimited resources to travel whenever and wherever I like.

I am truly grateful for the international opportunities that my business receives.

PATRICIA'S INSIGHTS:

While this section is about asking for help and energetic support, let me be clear. *You* need to know what you are calling in. There are a lot of people who will *want* to offer help and support, but not everyone will be the right person for you. There may also be people in your life who you *think* would offer you support but they won't.

Everyone has their opinion, a way of business that works best for them, advice on what you 'should' do. While their advice might be well-intentioned, what worked best for them might not be best for you. And that's okay!

There are two parts when it comes to asking for help. First is to acknowledge that you simply can't do this all on your own. In the beginning of my business, I had a VA who I was paying before I was even paying myself. She was doing all the things I couldn't do and she was just way more efficient and better at it than I was.

The second part is the help you get in your life. Like I mentioned, I hired a housekeeper. (In Bali, we also had a cleaner and full-time chef. Back in Ireland, I have someone who does my laundry because laundry is my nemesis! I love being able to open up my wardrobe where everything is clean and pressed.)

If you're just starting out with delegating, what $5 or $10 tasks could be outsourcing? Where can you ask for more help from community, friends, family, paid help or spiritual guides?

Outsourcing can be a conflicting topic, but it's how you get to run your business and life more efficiently. It also puts your money in the hands of good people, doing good things, while helping your impact in the world multiply. It gives you the spaciousness to dream and create, which is why so many successful business owners swear by it.

Don't concern yourself with negative people, especially the ones trying to bring you down. Being in business for yourself is an exciting but scary journey. Sometimes people pull you back because they think they are keeping you safe. Sometimes they are just doing it because your success highlights their own failure.

It's your job to discern who is a positive influence on you and who is not. Move away from those negative people and surround yourself with people who are supportive. Step away from people who are not changing and growing.

Being aware of what is going on around you is a good thing, but don't get bogged down in fear-based news about celebrities, politics or the economy. Keep your eyes on your vision, keep your energy clear, and let your results speak for themselves.

Speaking of results, it would be my recommendation not to do any free 'swaps' with anyone in terms of business. Besides the legal ramifications of not having a contract in place, swaps can be a dangerous way of influencing the energy of your business. Imagine yourself in five years where you are thriving in a successful business. Would you be swapping services rather than just paying for what you need? Surely, you'd be paying and hiring accordingly, so start with that energy now.

This is one of those areas where clear strong boundaries are needed from the beginning. It ensures the people in your sphere don't take advantage of you — because often swaps come with one person doing more than the other, or someone failing to deliver at all — and it protects your business. It shows the Universe the standards you are willing to accept.

Carla's Story

"SET IT. FORGET IT. AND THEN LAUGH WHEN YOU TELL THE NAYSAYERS YOU DID WARN THEM!"

I was working a job doing what I loved, but the job itself was not supportive of me. I had just bought my childhood home from my parents, which had stale energy about it, so I decided to do Patricia's PowerHouse programme.

After three months, I had around 80% of the remedies in place. At that point, my job was just horrible. I remember having the worst day. It was such a bad day that I walked out; I just realised I couldn't work there anymore. It was not sustainable.

By end of the following week, I had an interview. I was offered the job. I was ready to accept anything to get me out of the horrible job I had, but the new role ended up being extremely supportive. Plus, I've had a significant increase in income!

I'm now on a leadership team for a small group, and one of my intentions was that I wanted to be surrounded by people who are optimistic and helpful, where we are on the same page and don't have any issues. I'm happy to say that 99.9% of the time, we agree and move forward in the same direction. There's also massive growth within our group.

The great thing is you can start Patricia's work without spending lots of money on implementing the recommendations. A lot of the changes you can do are intentional and free. You don't have to go out and buy heaps of things to be able to Feng Shui your house effectively.

You can start with small steps, which I did. One of the remedies I liked doing was printing out a picture and putting it behind something already hanging on my wall. I set it and forget it! When I did that, I was invited to speak at a conference in the field I work in. They switched from an in-person event to a virtual event and I went from having 50 people at my speaking engagement to over 250 people from all over the world.

It's still on the internet and people talk about it even now. I've had interns from my previous company message me saying they found it and they'd like to talk to me about it. I get LinkedIn messages from across the globe because of those videos, all because I refused to move this picture from my wall that had the Feng Shui remedy on it.

You'll likely have naysayers in your life, as we all do. I still tell them I'm going to implement all the changes anyway and I see new growth every time without fail. Sometimes the naysayers in the team will complain about too much too fast and how we'll keep up. All I say to that is, "Well, I did warn you!"

PART 4

OTHER CONSIDERATIONS FOR YOUR OFFICE

Chapter Sixteen
YOUR POWER ELEMENT

Your power element and your power numbers can help you with your business, so let's dive into what exactly these are and how to use them. Power elements are made up of three things; an element, a power number and a power direction. Your power number determines which element, colours and directions are best for you. They are personal to you and completely separate from the Feng Shui of your office or home.

In Feng Shui, we work with the Five Elements: fire, water, wood, metal and earth. This is our biggest philosophy. Your power number will dictate which element is most strongly influential for you. Your power number will have a specific meaning and interpretation, which describes your general nature. You don't need to worry what the element is, because it is just an energetic form, so don't overthink it.

When it comes to your power element in your business and office, it's much more about making sure that you are sitting in the most helpful direction possible. The main use of knowing your element is to understand what will energise and deplete you. For example, if your element is fire — wearing green will fuel and enhance your energy, but a blue wall in your office will dampen your energy (and therefore your productivity). You don't have to avoid those elements entirely. Let's say water is the element that depletes you; that doesn't mean you can't go swimming. I'm saying your power element allows you to play to your strengths.

Power elements also tell you what your power colours are. For example, if your power number corresponds to the element of earth, then your power colour would be green; as such, it might serve you well to have a green wallet, or you might enjoy activities that involve nature. In essence, the earth element is your symbol and where you feel most at home. This is called your 'essence colour'.

What does all this mean for you and your business? Using your essence colour is super powerful because it helps you be more in your element and connect with your energy more deeply.

Some colours 'feed' your essence colour. For example, let's say you are a wood element. Wood represents anything that is green, such as plants. If you think about the element that a plant needs, you can determine that plants need water. So, if your element is wood and your essence colour is green, colours that feed you would correlate with water. I'll be sharing exactly what those colours are later in this chapter.

In addition to your essence colour, and the colour that feeds you, there are also colours that deplete you. Again, it is not necessary for you to be overly concerned about this. Don't go and change your whole branding based on this one colour! It's simply about being mindful of the colours that are supportive for you, and which ones might not be best when engaging in important events and activities for your business.

It's important to note that these colours are individual to you, not your space. Here, I'm not talking about the colours for your office, but the colours of your person. For example, if you are a fire element, and it is suggested that you wear red from time to time, or have a red wallet, this does not mean that you should paint your office wall red.

When it comes to business, your essence colour is a great colour for you to wear, to have as your logo, to use for your personal branding, and to use for your website or business card. It's also great for some of your personal items too, like a wallet or a handbag. In an important business meeting, by all means wear one of your essence or colours that feed you. I highly recommend this! If you are redesigning your entire website, look into a colour that feeds you and your essence colour. Any time you are putting yourself out into the world, that's when to use the colours that will bring you more energy. Essence colours can simply heighten your energy. You don't have to go overboard.

Then, just try to minimise or limit the colours that deplete you, because energetically that will be dulling the energy of your business.

Sometimes you might hate your essence colours. And that's okay! In Feng Shui, it's about finding what gets you into alignment and empowers you. Personal essence colours are just one way to do that.

Feng Shui is designed to help you create a positive relationship with your environment. Having all the elements in the office space Feng Shui-ed, with little pops of power colours, can make your environment feel better. The colours that feel good to you will also enhance your business, so do what resonates.

Now, let's calculate your power element.

How to calculate your power element

As the Chinese New Year runs from February 5th to February 5th each year, if you were born between January 1st and February 5th, you must subtract one year from your birth year.

Examples:

- If you were born on January 29th 2001, your power element year is 2000 for both males and females.
- If you were born on or after February 6th 2001, your power element year remains 2001 for both males and females.

Power element charts

Note: There is no number 5!

YEAR	M	F	ANIMAL
1940	6	9	Dragon
1941	2	1	Snake
1942	4	2	Horse
1943	3	3	Goat
1944	2	4	Monkey
1945	1	8	Rooster
1946	9	6	Dog
1947	8	7	Pig
1948	7	8	Rat
1949	6	9	Ox

YEAR	M	F	ANIMAL
1980	2	4	Monkey
1981	1	8	Rooster
1982	9	6	Dog
1983	8	7	Pig
1984	7	8	Rat
1985	6	9	Ox
1986	2	1	Tiger
1987	4	2	Rabbit
1988	3	3	Dragon
1989	2	4	Snake

YEAR	M	F	ANIMAL
2020	7	8	Rat
2021	6	9	Ox
2022	2	1	Tiger
2023	4	2	Rabbit
2024	3	3	Dragon
2025	2	4	Snake
2026	1	8	Horse
2027	9	6	Goat
2028	8	7	Monkey
2029	7	8	Rooster

YEAR	M	F	ANIMAL
1950	2	1	Tiger
1951	4	2	Rabbit
1952	3	3	Dragon
1953	2	4	Snake
1954	1	8	Horse
1955	9	6	Goat
1956	8	7	Monkey
1957	7	8	Rooster
1958	6	9	Dog
1959	2	1	Pig

YEAR	M	F	ANIMAL
1990	1	8	Horse
1991	9	6	Goat
1992	8	7	Monkey
1993	7	8	Rooster
1994	6	9	Dog
1995	2	1	Pig
1996	4	2	Rat
1997	3	3	Ox
1998	2	4	Tiger
1999	1	8	Rabbit

YEAR	M	F	ANIMAL
2030	6	9	Dog
2031	2	1	Pig
2032	4	2	Rat
2033	3	3	Ox
2034	2	4	Tiger
2035	1	8	Rabbit
2036	9	6	Dragon
2037	8	7	Snake
2038	7	8	Horse
2039	6	9	Goat

YEAR	M	F	ANIMAL
1920	8	7	Monkey
1921	7	8	Rooster
1922	6	9	Dog
1923	2	1	Pig
1924	4	2	Rat
1925	3	3	Ox
1926	2	4	Tiger
1927	1	8	Rabbit
1928	9	6	Dragon
1929	8	7	Snake

YEAR	M	F	ANIMAL
1960	4	2	Rat
1961	3	3	Ox
1962	2	4	Tiger
1963	1	8	Rabbit
1964	9	6	Dragon
1965	8	7	Snake
1966	7	8	Horse
1967	6	9	Goat
1968	2	1	Monkey
1969	4	2	Rooster

YEAR	M	F	ANIMAL
2000	9	6	Dragon
2001	8	7	Snake
2002	7	8	Horse
2003	6	9	Goat
2004	2	1	Monkey
2005	4	2	Rooster
2006	3	3	Dog
2007	2	4	Pig
2008	1	8	Rat
2009	9	6	Ox

YEAR	M	F	ANIMAL
1930	7	8	Horse
1931	6	9	Goat
1932	2	1	Monkey
1933	4	2	Rooster
1934	3	3	Dog
1935	2	4	Pig
1936	1	8	Rat
1937	9	6	Ox
1938	8	7	Tiger
1939	7	8	Rabbit

YEAR	M	F	ANIMAL
1970	3	3	Dog
1971	2	4	Pig
1972	1	8	Rat
1973	9	6	Ox
1974	8	7	Tiger
1975	7	8	Rabbit
1976	6	9	Dragon
1977	2	1	Snake
1978	4	2	Horse
1979	3	3	Goat

YEAR	M	F	ANIMAL
2010	8	7	Tiger
2011	7	8	Rabbit
2012	6	9	Dragon
2013	2	1	Snake
2014	4	2	Horse
2015	3	3	Goat
2016	2	4	Monkey
2017	1	8	Rooster
2018	9	6	Dog
2019	8	7	Pig

IF YOUR POWER NUMBER IS: 1

Your Element is **WATER**

Your Essence Colours are: **Blue and Black**

The Colours that FEED you are: **Gold, Silver, Copper and Grey**

The Colours that DEPLETE you are: **Earth tones, Browns, Yellows, Cream and Greens**

The Element that FEEDS you is: **METAL**

The Elements that DEPLETE you are: **WOOD and EARTH**

Your qualities are being flexible, yet focused and determined. You are empathetic, artistic and given to deep thought but tend to worry too much and may be overly sensitive.

Southeast (SE) is your Personal Best Direction. The best location for Prosperity and Great Fame. Have your back face this direction for productivity. The best location for the main breadwinner of the home to enter in.

East (E) is the best location for Great Health and Good Fortune. Good health location for the parents/elders of the home. Have your back face this direction while eating for better digestion.

South (S) is your best location for Family Harmony, Good Public Relationships and Longevity. Good health direction for the children in the home. This area improves family relationships and prevents arguments.

North (N) is your best location for Overall Harmony, Clarity (decision-making) and Peace. The best direction to place your headboard (so that the crown of your head faces this direction) to receive a good night's sleep. Good direction to sleep in and to help with fertility.

IF YOUR POWER NUMBER IS: 2

Your Element is **EARTH**

Your Essence Colours are: **Earth tones, Browns, Yellows, Cream**

The Colours that FEED you are: **Red, Purple, Burgundy, Burnt Orange, Bright Pink**

The Colours that DEPLETE you are: **Green, Gold, Silver, Copper and Grey**

The Element that FEEDS you is: **FIRE**

The Elements that DEPLETE you are: **METAL and WOOD**

Your qualities are that you are strong (often a caregiver) and can be a great leader, primarily in earthly matters.

Northeast (NE) is your Personal Best Direction. The best location for Prosperity and Great Fame. Have your back face this direction for productivity. The best location for the main breadwinner of the home to enter in.

West (W) is the best location for Great Health and Good Fortune. Good health location for the parents/elders of the home. Have your back face this direction while eating for better digestion.

Northwest (NW) is your best location for Family Harmony, Good Public Relationships and Longevity. Good health direction for the children in the home. This area improves family relationships and prevents arguments.

Southwest (SW) is your best location for Overall Harmony, Clarity (decision-making) and Peace. The best direction to place your headboard (so that the crown of your head faces this direction) to receive a good night's sleep. Good direction to help with fertility.

IF YOUR POWER NUMBER IS: 3

Your Element is **SOFT WOOD**

Your Essence Colours are: **Greens**

The Colours that FEED you are: **Black and Blue**

The Colours that DEPLETE you are: **Red, Purple, Burgundy, Burnt Orange, Bright Pink, Gold, Silver, Copper and Grey**

The Element that FEEDS you is: **WATER**

The Elements that DEPLETE you are: **FIRE and METAL**

Your qualities are being generally even-tempered but you can have sudden outbursts. You like to be moving and are not well-suited to a job where you have to sit still for long. You are enthusiastic and can be loud at times.

South (S) is your Personal Best Direction. The best location for Prosperity and Great Fame. Have your back face this direction for productivity. The best location for the main breadwinner of the home to enter in.

North (N) is the best location for Great Health and Good Fortune. Good health location for the parents/elders of the home. Have your back face this direction while eating for better digestion.

Southeast (SE) is your best location for Family Harmony, Good Public Relationships and Longevity. Good health direction for the children in the home. This area improves family relationships and prevents arguments.

East (E) is your best location for Overall Harmony, Clarity (decision-making) and Peace. The best direction to place your headboard (so that the crown of your head faces this direction) to receive a good night's sleep. Good direction to help with fertility.

IF YOUR POWER NUMBER IS: 4

Your Element is **HARD WOOD**

Your Essence Colours are: **Greens**

The Colours that FEED you are: **Black and Blue**

The Colours that DEPLETE you are: **Red, Purple, Burgundy, Burnt Orange, Bright Pink, Gold, Silver, Copper and Grey**

The Element that FEEDS you is: **WATER**

The Elements that DEPLETE you are: **FIRE and METAL**

Your qualities are being insightful and often driven but, like the wind's direction, you can change your mind abruptly and often. You tend to be creative and artistic.

North (N) is your Personal Best Direction. The best location for Prosperity and Great Fame. Have your back face this direction for productivity. The best location for the main breadwinner of the home to enter is.

South (S) is the best location for Great Health and Good Fortune. Good health location for the parents/elders of the home. Have your back face this direction while eating for better digestion.

East (E) is your best location for Family Harmony, Good Public Relationships and Longevity. Good health direction for the children in the home. This area improves family relationships and prevents arguments.

Southeast (SE) is your best location for Overall Harmony, Clarity (decision-making) and Peace. The best direction to place your headboard (so that the crown of your head faces this direction) to receive a good night's sleep. Good direction to help with fertility.

IF YOUR POWER NUMBER IS: 6

Your Element is **HARD METAL**

Your Essence Colours are: **Gold, Silver, Copper**

The Colours that FEED you are: **Earth tones, Browns, Yellows, Cream**

The Colours that DEPLETE you are: **Red, Purple, Burgundy, Burnt Orange, Bright Pink, Black and Blue**

The Element that FEEDS you is: **EARTH**

The Elements that DEPLETE you are: **WATER and FIRE**

Your qualities are being a natural-born leader and authority figure. However, you can be headstrong with strong masculine energy.

West (W) is your Personal Best Direction. The best location for Prosperity and Great Fame. Have your back face this direction for productivity. The best location for the main breadwinner of the home to enter in.

Northeast (NE) is the best location for Great Health and Good Fortune. Good health location for the parents/elders of the home. Have your back face this direction while eating for better digestion.

Southwest (SW) is your best location for Family Harmony, Good Public Relationships and Longevity. Good health direction for the children in the home. This area improves family relationships and prevents arguments.

Northwest (NW) is your best location for Overall Harmony, Clarity (decision-making) and Peace. The best direction to place your headboard (so that the crown of your head faces this direction) to receive a good night's sleep. Good direction to help with fertility.

IF YOUR POWER NUMBER IS: 7

Your Element is **SOFT METAL**

Your Essence Colours are: **Gold, Silver, Grey**

The Colours that FEED you are: **Earth tones, Browns, Yellows, Cream**

The Colours that DEPLETE you are: **Red, Purple, Burgundy, Burnt Orange, Bright Pink, Black and Blue**

The Element that FEEDS you is: **EARTH**

The Elements that DEPLETE you are: **WATER and FIRE**

Your qualities are being artistic, creative, sociable and talkative. You like things done right and you like to lead.

Northwest (NW) is your Personal Best Direction. The best location for Prosperity and Great Fame. Have your back face this direction for productivity. The best location for the main breadwinner of the home to enter in.

Southwest (SW) is the best location for Great Health and Good Fortune. Good health location for the parents/elders of the home. Have your back face this direction while eating for better digestion.

Northeast (NE) is your best location for Family Harmony, Good Public Relationships and Longevity. Good health direction for the children in the home. This area improves family relationships and prevents arguments.

West (W) is your best location for Overall Harmony, Clarity (decision-making) and Peace. The best direction to place your headboard (so that the crown of your head faces this direction) to receive a good night's sleep. Good direction to help with fertility.

IF YOUR POWER NUMBER IS: 8

Your Element is **EARTH**

Your Essence Colours are: **Earth tones, Yellows, Browns, Creams**

The Colours that FEED you are: **Red, Purple, Burgundy, Burnt Orange, Bright Pink**

The Colours that DEPLETE you are: **Greens, Black and Blue**

The Element that FEEDS you is: **FIRE**

The Elements that DEPLETE you are: **METAL and WOOD**

Your qualities are being stable, though you can be stubborn. You are youthful.

Southwest (SW) is your Personal Best Direction. The best location for Prosperity and Great Fame. Have your back face this direction for productivity. The best location for the main breadwinner of the home to enter in.

Northwest (NW) is the best location for Great Health and Good Fortune. Good health location for the parents/elders of the home. Have your back face this direction while eating for better digestion.

West (W) is your best location for Family Harmony, Good Public Relationships and Longevity. Good health direction for the children in the home. This area improves family relationships and prevents arguments.

Northeast (NE) is your best location for Overall Harmony, Clarity (decision-making) and Peace. The best direction to place your headboard (so that the crown of your head faces this direction) to receive a good night's sleep. Good direction to help with fertility.

IF YOUR POWER NUMBER IS: 9

Your Element is **FIRE**

Your Essence Colours are: **Red, Purple, Burgundy, Burnt Orange, Bright Pink**

The Colour that FEEDS you: **Green**

The Colours that DEPLETE you are: **Earth tones, Yellows, Browns, Creams, Black and Blue**

The Element that FEEDS you is: **WOOD**

The Elements that DEPLETE you are: **EARTH and WATER**

Your qualities are being extremely active, sometimes to the point of becoming ill or burning yourself out. You are passionate; however, you can be hot-tempered.

East (E) is your Personal Best Direction. The best location for Prosperity and Great Fame. Have your back face this direction for productivity. The best location for the main breadwinner of the home to enter in.

Southeast (SE) is the best location for Great Health and Good Fortune. Good health location for the parents/elders of the home. Have your back face this direction while eating for better digestion.

North (N) is your best location for Family Harmony, Good Public Relationships and Longevity. Good health direction for the children in the home. This area improves family relationships and prevents arguments.

South (S) is your best location for Overall Harmony, Clarity (decision-making) and Peace. The best direction to place your headboard (so that the crown of your head faces this direction) to receive a good night's sleep. Good direction to help with fertility.

Power element colours are so powerful for your branding, because design and colour psychology can impact how you and others feel. Branding is a great way to create harmony between the conscious and unconscious cues that make a client decide whether you are trustworthy and credible. That harmony is also what we work with in Feng Shui, that yin and yang of conscious and unconscious energy in your space. It all needs to feel like it belongs together.

Now that you've explored your personal power number, considered your best directions, as well as colours and elements that feed and deplete you, let's take a look at how you can implement this new understanding.

Chapter Seventeen

OFFICE, CHAIR AND DESK POSITIONING

Improving the flow of energy in the Power Centres is just one way to introduce Feng Shui to your home. In this chapter, we will look at some more Feng Shui best practices for your office. Not everyone has a huge office space or even a dedicated room in their house. Ken and I travel so much that we often end up having to share an office. When these things happen, I like to have some Feng Shui basics in my back pocket to make the best of the space we have. You can apply these principles even if all you have is a desk.

Desk positioning

When it comes to desk positioning, it doesn't matter where your office is set up, because the most important factor is making sure your desk is aligned with you.

In the last section, I explained how to calculate your power element, which will give you your four power directions. It helps you calculate your most auspicious places to sit for productivity, health, career and sleep. Ideally, you'll sit with your back to the wall and make sure that the wall is in one of these four power directions.

You can even use these directions when you're going to a meeting, for example. Say you get there a little bit early and there is a big conference table for you to sit around. You can get your compass on your phone out and pick the best direction for you.

Now you may not be able to sit in your power direction. Every room is different. However, try to position yourself with a strong wall behind you and make sure you can see the door. Those are the two foundational pieces to positioning yourself and your desk. This is what we call your power position rather than your power direction.

Oftentimes, desks are jammed into the corner or pushed up to the wall. This isn't ideal because it may signify feeling cornered or having a sense of going nowhere. You also don't want your desk facing a wall because that represents coming up against a lot of frustrations and pushing up against things you can't see.

If you can, move your desk out from the wall and sit with your back to a wall, with space in front of you. This gives you a sense of expansion. Being able to see the door also brings a feeling of spaciousness.

If you don't have a strong wall behind you, a screen will work too. Another option and my personal favourite is a good tall chair! An 'I'm the boss' chair that has a high back is super supportive. I cannot reiterate enough how a comfortable, strong chair is *vital* for your alignment!

What if you have to sit with your back to the door? The way around this is placing a small mirror on your desk, so that you can still see the door opening and anyone coming in. This will make a big difference. And what about if you have your back to a window? This is an unsupportive position because windows are fickle and can break easily. The previous suggestion of a high back chair or screen will help here too.

I've worked with clients who have been sitting with their back to the door. When I walk in and they have their back to me as they would to a client, it's a vulnerable position. I asked one client if she was feeling overwhelmed with everything going on "Is everything landing on your shoulders? Does it feel like it comes out of nowhere? Have you been stressed out?" She burst into tears.

"How did you know?" she asked. It was simple. It was all down to the way she was sitting. This woman was the director of the company and completely overwhelmed with what was landing on her desk. She couldn't see coming — *because her back was to the door.*

Lastly, make sure your desk is not positioned under any exposed beams. Sitting under low beams for any length of time is a negative symbol in Feng Shui because it signifies having a lot of pressure on you. If you have been under an exposed beam, you might be feeling the weight of your responsibilities physically pressing you down or that someone is putting a lot of pressure upon you. And if the beam is split, it could cause your energy to split; which is going to cause anxiety, stress and tension. Three things you definitely don't want if you're trying to work productively!

Other fun Feng Shui tips

1. Desks should not be placed directly in front of a window, as this can be distracting.
2. Desks should not face a toilet door.
3. Desks should be made out of wood.
4. Desks should not be placed under exposed beams or spotlights.
5. The ideal shape of a desk is rounded at the front, if possible, to avoid corners pointing at anyone who approaches the desk.
6. Arrange desks facing the same direction to avoid office politics where possible.

Your view

As well as facing the door, consider what else you see from your seat, especially looking out of the office windows. When I'm teaching Feng Shui for homes, one of the first principles is keeping the windows nice and clean. You want to see opportunities clearly approaching you, not look out onto murky lands through dirty windows.

If your view is one of overflowing rubbish bins, what does that say about what you are expecting as you share your mission with the world? Every single element that affects your senses affects how you internally and subconsciously read that energy. That's why it's so important to have resonant images and items in your eye line. These contribute to the vibrancy of your life, your business and your mission.

Be super vigilant about the imagery of your office. Put your vision board somewhere within your eye line if you can, or choose images that represent abundance and prosperity to you. The upcoming chapter on artwork will also be useful.

Cubicle Feng Shui

What about if you are in a large office that has cubicles or desk separators? What do you do about your Feng Shui then? You could choose to Feng Shui your desk according to the nine Power Centres on a micro level, or you could use some of these best practices.

The first and most important priority is to make sure you can see the entrance to your cube from your desk. Get yourself in a powerful and empowered position. If you can't see the entrance to your cubicle when you are working at your desk, place a mirror somewhere in front of you so you can see the reflection of the door or opening.

Make sure your workspace is pleasing to your eye, uncluttered and comfortable to work in. Consider using a curved keyboard designed to be easy on the hands and wrists. Choose an optical scan mouse that allows you to scroll more easily and that doesn't require a mouse pad — you can do without the clutter.

Bring living and flowing energy into your workspace. Adding a plant into this space can help you stimulate more active, vibrant energy. Install full-spectrum lighting instead of fluorescent lights if you can. Avoid sharp angles pointing at people as they create attacking energy. These features are important ways of compensating for the small size of your space and the constant traffic flows that pass by your cube.

Most probably, your cubicle will not have any windows to let you see the outside world. In such a case, you can hang some pictures of landscapes on the walls. It creates the illusion of windows, will help the flow of good chichi, and should also make you feel relaxed and at ease.

Ensure that your cubicle is clean and free of any dust and rubbish. From cabinets and drawers to monitors and keyboards, everything should be free of dirt. As a cleaning solution, you can use a natural combination of water, vinegar and tea tree oil. When it comes to decluttering, discard everything that you do not need and will not require in the future.

Finally, create a couple of employment goals and decide which aspects of your career you would like to enhance. Keep this simple. Focus on one or two improvements at a time. Now, make those goals the intention of your cubby and make a firm commitment to yourself to achieve these goals.

Sharing an office

When it comes to sharing an office, whether that's with a lot of people or even just with your spouse at home, you're not always going to get the best positioning. In fact, you might end up with the worst seat in the house. You just have to work with what you've got.

Everyone has their own power element, the four best directions that are right for them, as we explored in the last chapter. If you run a large company and get a Feng Shui expert to come in and do a business consultation, they should also calculate the power elements of your team and do their best to account for at least one of the power directions for each member if they can. The power element is designed to help each member play to their strengths.

Of course, some team members will likely have opposite directions. Ken and I do! While travelling, that means we need to decide who gets what power direction in which room. In our bedroom, the bed is set up in Ken's power direction. When we share an office, it is set up in my power direction. It will be up to you what you feel is best when you consider your power elements from the last chapter, but just know it's not the be all and end all if you don't sit in your power direction.

Here are some other best practices to put in place.

First, if you can, make sure your office is dedicated to work and only work. I've been into so many offices that have suitcases, exercise equipment, books and other *stuff* irrelevant to work. This is your *workspace*. Treat it as such. Anything that's not work-related gets decluttered!

Second, get good, solid furniture that is comfortable and supports you. I had a white chair on my vision board for a long time before I bought it. Now I absolutely adore that chair. It not only feels comfortable but it gives me that sense of support behind me. And I have a solid, spacious desk too. There's not much on the desk and it feels clear. This gives me a sense of clarity and spaciousness to try new things.

If you share your office, have a think about what could make your office super comfortable for everyone. Brainstorm together. When Ken and I moved into our latest office, we noticed the floor was quite cold sometimes. So, I got this gorgeous warm rug under our feet. I love it. It makes me *want* to walk into my office in the morning. When I walk in, my toes feel cosy. Think about what could bring you more comfort so you would want to spend more time in your workspace, but also what would spark joy and excitement, what would make you want to sit at your desk, in your chair, spending time creating and working with your team.

Remember, this is *the* place where you work with your clients, send invoices, do your calls and push out your marketing campaigns. Do you want it to feel like an inspiring place or a lacklustre one? I invite you to think about what you would do if you had clients coming to visit tomorrow. How would you set it up? How would you change it? What would you have in it? What would you quickly get rid of?! I bet you'd do some things differently and you'd place items in the space to inspire and uplift.

Create *that* space and watch how it brings your dream client in, regardless of whether they visit in person or not.

Is the energy in your office just right?

How can you tell when your office is in good energy? This is a question I'm asked a lot. It's about making sure that the energy is moving around. That there's a sense of flow.

The first step is making sure you clear out stuff in your desk and your office that isn't relevant to your work or intentions. By all means, you can keep a picture of your family if that's why you started your business and you can keep any changes you've made as recommended in this book. What you're clearing here is anything that isn't intentionally selected for your business — or items from the past that have snuck back in.

When I was Feng Shui-ing cubicles in America, there was one woman whose cubicle was covered in fluffy toys. Even she said, "God, it looks like I don't take my job seriously."

If you've done your decluttering and still have some related work *stuff* you need to tidy away, take a look at your storage options. You will likely have to keep some files for legal purposes and probably some books for reference. I recommend enclosed neatly organised storage. If you have a choice between open shelves and covered storage, I would pick the latter. Here are my three top tips when it comes to storage:

1. Align books at the edge of bookshelves.
2. Keep files in storage, labelled clearly and colour-coded.
3. Minimise open shelving units as these can lead to distraction and clutter.

Then look at your desk positioning, which I talked about at the beginning of this chapter. Can you see the door? Are you under any low ceilings? Where are you positioned in relation to the walls? Taking all that together, what is the best place to sit in the space you have?

Next, add inspiration to your office to make it as productive, creative and inspirational as possible. That could be something living like a soft fern or a money plant. Whatever it is, it should be healthy, thriving and cared for. It needs to be looked after well, like your business. In this step, you can personalise the additions you make to meet your needs and those of your team. You want to create a place where you feel happy, calm or excited to spend a lot of time in!

I have a red cushion on my office chair, because red is a good fit for me energetically and a good match for the energy of the office too. It's a great colour to feel energised. Have a think about what you can bring in from the helpful colours you identified in the last chapter.

We spend so much time in our offices, especially if we work from home, but sometimes they can be neglected. This affects your vibrancy, productivity and creativity in business. Eliminate everything that no longer serves where you know the business is going and build yourself a space that is perfectly uplifting and in alignment with your next step.

Chapter Eighteen

DECORATING YOUR OFFICE WITH ART

Art is crazy powerful in Feng Shui. Unbeknown to you, the art you have around you impacts what you manifest in your life, because of all the time you spend in your office being influenced by it.

I can't stress enough the importance of art in the office and its effect on your subconscious mind. That's why it's important to have art around you that inspires you, makes you feel supported and productive! So, what's on your wall?

When it comes to choosing artwork, you may have already picked up a few suggestions throughout this book, but also trust your instinct. Keep being true to yourself and pick out things that remind you of your business, why you got started and what spurs you on.

I have this lovely piece of art in my office with hummingbirds on it that one of my amazing clients made for me. I also have a rainbow unicorn with the quote: *Today is going to be an amazing day!* Then there's this beautiful picture of trees in a field of bluebells that hangs on the wall in my office. I've had this piece for years and years. I absolutely love it! Now, these might not be inspiring for you, but they resonate with me.

Artwork that resonates is one of the most common suggestions I make to clients. That doesn't mean you have to run out and get a picture of bluebells for your office. However, consider the symbolism in artwork because that is powerful.

You want pieces of art that represent growth and abundance, flourishing and expansion. In the case of my bluebell picture, trees represent growth, reaching upward towards the sun! Beneath them is this massive bed of bluebells. Now, you never see one bluebell on its own, so that's your energy of abundance, growth and expansion.

You might choose a family photo for your desk. That's a good reminder of who you are working to provide for and why you're doing this. If you work with a team, it can also be a great idea to have a team photo as well.

You may want to keep your walls clear so that lots of fresh opportunities can come to you. Sometimes, you might choose to put your mission statement, goals or vision board on the blank wall. The vision board you have been cultivating through this book will be your visual representation of all the things you want your business to be and do, and the things you want to have in your life. If it's hanging on your wall, it becomes a daily reminder of your intention, something that you can look at every single day to remind you of your deepest desires. And that's powerful.

Attention is powerful: where your attention goes, your energy flows, so you want your attention focused on everything you want to attract into your life, right? Creating a powerful vision of where you are going will make you more energised and give you more momentum to move forward.

The best Feng Shui art is the art that brings you a vibrant quality of energy that lifts and nourishes you. Art is an excellent way to help create the symbols and images needed to bring good chi to you.

I've seen art that has held people back in their offices and businesses. One of my clients had a picture of a gloomy winter scene as a piece of artwork on her walls. When I ask people what they want in their business, money is usually the top priority. Does a dark wintery scene represent the season of abundance? No! What was worse in this example is that the picture was a gift from her ex-husband, so it held the energy of something that hadn't worked out. Double no-no!

Another client wanted a windfall, but all of his pictures were of this lovely, quiet, scenic place in Ireland. The images were so relaxing, so I wasn't surprised when he told me he sometimes came into his office to watch Netflix. That wasn't the energy he needed to get his windfall!

The art you want should represent flow, movement or growth. Whether life imitates art or art imitates life, be sure that the art you choose to have in your environment is art that reflects the kind of life you want to enjoy. The art might also represent your business values and resonate with the joy of what you are choosing for your life today.

POWERHOUSE PRACTICE: Art assessment

Now you know the influence art has on Feng Shui, take a look around your office and get an overall sense of the imagery you're bringing into the space and the energy it has.

What does your choice of artworks say about you?

Do you feel inspired when you look at the art in your workspace?

Do your artworks still reflect who you are right now?

Does the art in your office reflect where you are in business right now or where you want to go?

Evaluate these pieces one by one. Look at the artwork on your office walls and decide what stays and what goes. Ask yourself:

What do you want to create for your business and why?

Does a particular artwork inspire you to achieve that?

Does it resonate with where your business is going?

If the art no longer fits who you are right now and the life you have chosen to lead, then it needs to leave your environment. If there is a photo or painting in your office that you do not like or that reminds you of someone or somewhere you don't like, remove it!

Art to avoid

As well as any pieces that no longer mirror the energy you want for your business, you may also want to avoid:

- People sleeping or with their eyes closed. You wouldn't want people sleeping on the job! There's a difference between relaxing and creating a warm environment and making your staff sleepy. (Unless you work in a spa, in which case, these types of pictures would be great!)
- Solitary items. One flower in its own vase, one boat floating in the ocean, a person by themselves — these all symbolise being all alone. No one can run a business completely alone, so you don't want these.
- Boats tied up. These are a sign of going nowhere.
- Stormy scenes. Imagine what this signifies!
- Mountains: This represents an uphill struggle.

Even the placement of art can make a difference. One of my clients used to walk down her hallway to her office and all you saw was this picture of a mountain. So, I said to her, "Does it feel like an uphill battle before you've even started your day?" When she confirmed it did, we moved the mountain to the side wall in the hallway so she could feel the support of the mountain instead.

This rule isn't set in stone. Remember, it's about the intention! Art is personal. As a general rule, Feng Shui consultants will tell you not to showcase knives or guns, because weapons can symbolise tensions. However, for a certain Hollywood director having his office Feng-Shui-ed, that wasn't the case.

When the Feng Shui consultant arrived in his office, the first thing she noticed was the massive picture of a gun. The consultant asked, "What does this picture mean to you?" The director got so excited and explained, "This was the first movie I directed. It was the biggest success and *my* biggest success." He raved about the movie it represented. And the Feng Shui consultant told him to keep the gun picture.

You see, that picture was not about the gun. To the Hollywood director, that picture was about success. It reminded him of his success, his career, of keeping going, of enjoying the journey, of joy and positive energy. That's what I mean when I say art is personal.

That's also why, when I suggest avoiding some imagery, I'm not telling you to get rid of all the art you may already have. I'm not saying you should go and declutter all of the pictures of sleeping people, single people, boats tied up, or stormy scenes. Just reflect on what each piece means to you. Understand that a stormy scene in your prosperity area could make it a rough ride when it comes to wealth. If you've spent a lot of money on paintings or invested in art, make sure that artwork is sparking joy.

Chapter Nineteen

IF YOUR OFFICE IS ANOTHER ROOM IN YOUR HOUSE

If there is no dedicated office space in your home, don't be discouraged. When your workspace is another room in your house, Feng Shui can still work for you! The key is to create some boundaries. This is important not just from a Feng Shui perspective, but also for your sanity! It can be so tempting when we are working from home to 'just check that email' after dinner or log on to social media and start answering messages from your clients. A lack of boundaries sets a standard of expectation that will eventually burn you out!

No matter where your workspace is — whether it's your bedroom, your kitchen, your living room, or even in the toilets — take note of the following tips.

First, check your power position. Can you get yourself into your power position, facing the door and with your back to a wall. This is different to your power direction, but you should try to have both a power position and your power direction in play if possible.

Secondly, change up the space you're working in a little so there's a different energy in the room when it is 'work time' versus when the room is used for other things. It's about intentionality, right? If you're working from the kitchen table, clear off everything that's not work-related when you sit down to begin your day. Put your laptop there or something else that kind of anchors work for you. It could be a notepad, a particular coffee mug, anything you choose. At the end of the day, when it's time to finish, close your laptop and put away the items that have anchored you into your working day. Then pull out some table mats or reset the table with place settings and you'll change the environment!

I had one client who lived in this tiny studio apartment in New York. She lived and worked there, running a multiple six-figure business from that apartment. Her bedroom was her office and her living room. It was all combined in one. Still, we managed to make it work for her Feng Shui.

First, we focused on putting her in a power position. Then we made sure she had a different set of cushions on her bed at night-time than she did during the day when it was a pull-out couch. She had different throws and cushions to make the room into a living room when she got up in the morning. At night, she would cover her laptop and desk with the night-time throw and then she'd pull out and make her bed with the other cushions. This might seem like a lot of work, but it was a complete transformation that allowed her to reset her energy and take care of her business as well as her personal time off.

During the day, you would never know that apartment was her bedroom! At night, you'd assume she worked and lived somewhere else. These are the clear boundaries I'm talking about working with from a physical sense. You have to change it up a bit.

Another client could see her office desk from her bedroom every night before she went to sleep. She told me she was overwhelmed with running an international company that received messages all through the night. Shifting this overwhelm was as simple as putting a closed sign on her desk when she was finished for the day and shutting her bedroom door at night so she couldn't see her workspace.

Particularly when you're working from home, it's important to be able to switch off. Another of my clients bought an 'open' and 'closed' sign to hang on her office door. Every Friday, she would change the sign to closed. This gave her the space in her life to not only call in love but also her dream business partner too!

It's the little intentional things that can make a huge impact. Look for simple ways to change up your space and you can still reap the rewards of Feng Shui.

Chapter Twenty

DOS AND DON'TS IN FENG SHUI FOR BUSINESS

As well as having items around you that inspire you, encourage you and make you feel comfortable, here are a few more considerations that you may need to make, depending on your office space.

Do: Keep on cleaning
Don't: Think there's nothing left to do

Remember I suggested cleaning your windows and front door? These are going to keep getting dirty and will need to be cleaned on an ongoing basis. If something is not working in your business, and you've gone through this book and done all you can, the entrance of your office may hold the key. It's where you should spend your time if nothing feels like it's working. The more effort and energy you spend at the mouth of your office, the more your office will love you, welcome in new energy, and feel that chi entering.

While you clean, express gratitude because with gratitude comes acknowledgement and appreciation. When you are grateful for what you have already received, you'll notice more. So, give thanks for even the tiniest blessings.

Abundance mindset and attraction work closely together in Feng Shui. When you have ample money, give as generously as you can. When you don't have ample money to share, you can still give your time, energy, compassion, appreciation, or gratitude. Give with the power of your thoughts, so that you're able to reap the rewards.

Do: Keep prosperous plants
Don't: Have fake flowers!

We've touched on which plants to introduce to your office, but don't forget to water and care for them! Also, remove dead plants, dead flowers, dried flowers or silk flowers. These all represent dead energy. They are not recommended in any Feng Shui, because they are stagnant, hold on to past energy, and have no life around them.

Do: Look for clues
Don't: Ignore signs

Your office is giving you clues about where you can become more prosperous or stop draining your energy. Notice where bulbs burn out and replace them. You may notice a pattern and see that the areas where bulbs burn out correspond to places in your life and business where you are dimming your own energy. There will be something exhausting you in that area. Burnt-out bulbs are giving you a sign. Think what that sign could mean.

Do: Keep your office in working order
Don't: Keep broken things around

If you want money flowing into your business, keep all items around the office working! It can be tempting to just keep 'getting by' and save on costs where you can, but broken energy comes from broken stuff. If your office desk or office chair is broken, those are significant items to fix or replace! If it's unable to be repaired, let it go!

Try to keep in mind that everything is replaceable, like breathing in and out. At any moment, you are able to inhale and bring in new energy. Then exhale and let it all go. All the time, every moment, new things are coming. All the time, every moment, the old is being let go. Allow yourself to step into that abundant mindset when releasing anything broken, cracked, or chipped if it can't be repaired.

Tighten loose door knobs or handles, and make sure you have handles on your doors. Drawer handles are such tiny little things and easily overlooked, but each time you go to use a frustrating broken handle, it depletes your energy. When you get annoyed trying to open a stuck drawer or use a broken handle, this speaks to you getting a grip on your finances and your life. It's about how you handle yourself and anything that comes your way. Repair all door knobs or handles, and make sure they're solid.

Do: Take care of your finances
Don't: Treat your money like an object

Your finances symbolise all money in your life. If you don't have an accountant managing your business finances, make sure to balance your accounts regularly. Pay your bills on time. Chase for invoices. Check your bank accounts as a matter of habit. This 'shows' money that you care about your relationship with it more than giving it a needy 'more, more, more' energy. Think of your relationship with money like a partnership and nurture it like any other.

Other considerations for bigger office buildings

Whether you are already in a commercial office building, or considering expanding into another office building, here are some of the tips that a Feng Shui consultant would be considering when weighing up which property is right for you and your business. If you can't control any of these things, just do what you can. These are nice-to-have extras in Feng Shui!

- If there is another business across the way, then your office entrance should not be smaller than the other business's entrance.
- Always keep the customers coming in the right side door, and out the left side door.
- The main entrance should be well lit, well marked and free of obstacles.
- The reception area should be warm and welcoming. The receptionist should not be in the direct line of the entrance — this is too much chi and the receptionist may not last long in the position.
- Ceilings or walls that seep water or are cracked from moisture can indicate a financial loss. Get them fixed!
- Ceilings should be high. If ceilings are too low, this will create a feeling of pressure and can hinder the progress of the business.
- The office of the boss should not be next to a water tap as this could lead to financial loss.
- The office of the highest authority should be located furthest from the front entrance.
- It is best when office doors do not open directly across from each other.

HAZEL'S STORY:

"I CAN ACCOUNT FOR AN EXTRA $200,000 USD SINCE I STARTED DOING FENG SHUI."

I have been a registered nurse at Mass General Hospital for 35 years and I've also held my real estate licence for the last 2.5 years.

I was intrigued by Feng Shui, but like many people, I thought it was all about moving furniture around. Then I did Patricia's first masterclass. I made every change she told me to, keeping the toilet seat down to having coins in the abundance corner. My children thought I was crazy but within weeks my son won $67,000 in a lottery. It was amazing!

After that, I decided to do PowerHouse. I set my intention: I wanted to be recognised as a nurse and in real estate. I'd been in the programme for about seven months when I was told I was one of the top ten realtors in our company, which has over 100 realtors. I also got a $27,000 commission from a condo I sold. Here I am as a full-time nurse doing this!

At the same time, I was asked by Mass General to speak to a group of medical students about a huge project that I've been doing. This was recognition, which to me meant more than money.

Then I got a $2,000 check from an attorney closing a previous real estate deal *and* a medical refund of $15,100. To top it all off, I manifested my dream house overlooking the Boston skyline and waterfront.

When I moved in, I knew the house was neglected and I needed to fix it. I talked to my house and said out loud, "Please bring the money in easily so I can fix this house because there are lots of projects I want to do."

The project I was doing ended up giving me 10 hours of overtime a week. And because I've been a nurse for 35 years and this was time and a half, I earned an extra $120 an hour. Initially, I had not cared how long the project would last. I thought it would be a month or two. However, I kept putting my intentions on my little index cards in my career area, and that overtime lasted for one full year. That's over $1,000 USD on my pay cheque every week for the last 12 months.

The amount I earned from overtime was the exact same amount as the total cost of all the projects I wanted to do on the new house. I was blown away because that just doesn't happen to nurses. People kept asking me how I was getting all this overtime every week and I said, "it's my Feng Shui." I can account for an extra $200,000 USD since I started doing Feng Shui.

CHAPTER TWENTY-ONE

FENG SHUI FOR YOUR WEBSITE

Having worked in my family's brick-and-mortar businesses, sold my own cakes and trinkets at the Galway market as a teenager and then run a holistic business for a couple of years in Ireland, I've learnt a lot about the difference between an offline business versus an online one. Someone once asked me what I would focus on if I was starting my business from scratch. My answer is always that there's no right or wrong — that's not the most helpful way of looking at business.

The reason I was asked to leave my family business was because it was obvious to everyone that I needed to fulfil my own dreams. I didn't know what I wanted but I needed a big change. My mum had always said to me that I was always ready to go on an adventure. Apparently, I would sense someone was going out and I'd put a coat on, ready to go.

When I moved back from India, I unknowingly set up a business that didn't give me freedom, my core value. Even though I didn't want any team members, I ended up building a business where I was working with people one-on-one, in meditation circles, and other events like that. I thought to myself, "Oh no. What have I done? Everything is in person. I don't have the freedom to travel."

When I realised how powerful Feng Shui was for my life and my business, I made an intentional decision to build an online business. Ken and I went away for our honeymoon and that lifestyle kept going for several years. I sold everything and let go of my bricks and mortar business. I didn't have a clue what I was doing online, but I pivoted anyway.

The lesson I've learnt is that there's no right or wrong in your business. You choose what you want. I still love in-person business! I love the people I meet. My online business now has in-person elements too, such as retreats in Bali, events around the world. It's about personal choice and what feels best. One of my highest values is freedom, so building a business that allowed me to travel was important.

Once in Bali, my online business grew considerably over the three years that followed. There are many lessons and so much growth to share from that experience and I hope you've learnt a lot through these chapters.

Seeing as I've spent so long of this book telling you about how Feng Shui has been revolutionary to my business, you might be wondering how I did it while travelling. And while, yes, I did Feng Shui every house Ken and I stayed in, I also Feng Shui-ed my website, which was a constant no matter where I went in the world.

Feng Shui your virtual home

Your website is your virtual home, but it's not like each area of your website has to match a certain Power Centre. Still, the lessons that we've covered can be applied to your online home and presence too.

The Health Centre

Look into your website functionality. Do all the buttons work? Are there any 404 links or broken pages? How fast does your website page load? Is your website responsive to mobile and tablet as well as desktop? Making sure your website is in peak condition shows current and future clients that you are serious about your business and that you have an established base. Taking time out of your business every year to make sure everything is up to date and working at peak efficiency is like having a spring clean for your home! It will refresh the energy and attract new people to it.

The Career and Business Mission Centre

Is your business mission on your website? Do people actually know what you *do*? What do you stand for? What are your values? I see so many websites where they think that what the business does is clear but it doesn't actually spell it out. Sometimes the images don't match what the business is trying to communicate. Have a look at the vision board you've been creating throughout this book and then at your website. Do the pictures you've picked for the vision board and the website align with where you want the business to go? Do they align with those clear values you've established? Your business mission is your statement to the world. It's how you introduce yourself. You should have it front and centre on your homepage.

The Knowledge and Skills Centre

What do you want to learn next when it comes to your website or online presence? You may be learning how to build your website yourself or have someone do it for you, but what's next? How can you improve and enhance your online presence to help grow your business? It could even be as simple as learning to run a Facebook group or mastering your fear of going live online.

The Teamwork, Growth and New Beginnings Centre

Do you have a section where new website visitors get to meet your team if you have one? People buy people, which means they have to know, like and trust you. If you don't want to be doing it all by yourself, or you don't want the entire business reputation to rely on you showing up live on social media every day, you should consider introducing your team to the world. Let them have a little section where they can share some fun facts on your website, or allow them to take over your business social media so that your audience can build rapport with your team too.

The Prosperity and Power Centre

How much traffic do you have coming to your website? If you don't know how to track this, how do you know how well your marketing is performing? How do you know how to call in *more* traffic if you have no idea which channels are bringing in visitors? Get up to speed with your website analytics, learn what's working for you and what's not. Then you'll know where to place your energy and intention to boost your website visits to the prosperous number you have in mind!

The Fame and Reputation Centre

Part of the reputation centre is about branding, which is where those power element colours come in if you're willing to use them. Take some time to go over your branding and see if it's going in the same direction as your business, or if it can grow with you. This is also the area where people will look for your 'social proof' banner. What magazines, podcasts or well-known places have you been featured? Having a social proof banner on your homepage is great for your online reputation!

The Business Partners Centre

Reputation goes beyond your own site. It's also about who you're connected to online, which means backlinks. All your online media should have backlinks, which will drive more people to your website and helps with your website's search engine optimisation. The more backlinks you have with reputable media partners, the higher you rank on the likes of Google! This is also the centre where we consider your testimonials. Do you have any on your website? Are they easy to find? You may also choose to have a banner representing the other people and businesses you work with. Again, this is great for backlinks and proof that people trust you and work with you in the online space.

The Creativity, Communication, Marketing and Productivity Centre

On your website, this theme relates to the strength of your website copy! Are your messages clear and compelling? Do they speak to your ideal client, empathise with them and then give them the solution to their problem or show them how to get from A to B? Do you give them examples and results in the form of testimonials? Get a content marketer, someone in your team, or a client you trust to have a read over your main web pages and spot any holes in your messaging.

The Helpful People and Travel Centre

How helpful is your website? Is it clear to see where you're located or how to get in touch with you? Are there any restrictions to the countries you work in online and where customers are situated? Is it all online? With so many businesses being international and online these days, you want to be transparent about where you're located and how people can get in touch to work with you. I'm amazed at the number of websites where there's no clear signposting around how to get in touch with someone from the business. You may opt for a simple contact form, but many people are now turned off by these as so many businesses don't get back to them. So, my suggestion is always a page called 'Contact' in your menu bar that then has a list of your team and who to get in touch with for what.

If you want to take it one step further, I recommend sending an automated email thanking them for their message and stating when they can expect to hear from you. For example, I tell anyone who emails me that I check my emails once a day between Tuesday and Thursday. That way they have clear expectations from the beginning and you're starting your business relationship off on the right foot!

PART 5

THE POWER OF FENG SHUI IN YOUR BUSINESS

Chapter Twenty-Two

BIG OBSTACLES TO FENG SHUI'ING YOUR BUSINESS

Starting out with Feng Shui can be a bit daunting but don't worry. Here, I'll cover the big obstacles that you may come up against now or in the future.

Too much information

When I first started sharing Feng Shui, I would go to the client's house, do the walk around, have their floor plan, give them advice, analyse the numbers, and tell them everything they needed to know in like three to four hours. It was too much information all in one go! They never did the homework. They could have emailed me, but none of my clients followed through and implemented the recommended additions. That's when I learnt: implementation gets results.

If you don't practice an instrument, you're not going to be able to play it! It's the same with Feng Shui. It's a practice. It's why I broke down the steps you can take into small bite-sized exercises. It's also why I built my PowerHouse programme and our community that gives people the chance to ask their Feng Shui questions seven days a week. Feng Shui is a process, so it's natural for questions to pop up at random intervals. People in our community are delighted at having their questions answered quickly. It's also a great way to get support, advice and encouragement from other people who are in a similar boat to you as you continue this journey.

No proper guidance

To be honest, when I started my business I used to just try to figure it out from googling and watching what others did online, this is where people trying to implement 'figure feng shui out alone' go wrong. Then I invested in courses to teach me how to do it properly and that was a game changer. We learned so much by following a plan that someone has done before. Ken and I watched all the videos, did all the homework, we followed through on *everything*. And got the results.

That's also my advice with this book. Do *everything*. Follow through. I've given you all the basics of using Feng Shui in your business so that it can be the launchpad for you too. And then, when you get confident, have a play! The most important thing is trusting what feels good to you. It's why I've been asking you to answer these questions for yourself and make your Feng Shui bespoke to you.

Bespoke plans and inner belief

When I saw my clients' life-changing results in PowerHouse, I upgraded the programme to a version where they would get a personal report. My business grew exponentially from there, because clients don't have to do the hard work of figuring out what's wrong and learning how to fix it.

If you have even a tiny inkling it won't work for you, it still will! You've heard about a lot of sceptical husbands in this book who are converted! However, if you have belief that it will amplify your results, it's even more powerful. It's your belief that drives this. I didn't give you a cookie-cutter approach, because business and Feng Shui doesn't work like that. What works for one doesn't work for another because belief and intention play *such* a huge part in the process.

Losing momentum

Momentum is also about your own belief. Let's take advertising as an example. If you believe ads work, they'll work. If you buy into the stories that ads don't work, then they won't. This is why some people succeed with paid advertising, others do incredible things with organic reach, and some have huge success with five-day challenges. It's all about what they can get behind, believe and give their all.

Give gratitude to what works for you. I thank Facebook every day that they have a platform that allows me to advertise in a way that works for us and can be a place I build my community. That gratitude energy keeps that platform working for me. You know what I'm going to say — it's the same with Feng Shui!

We can get excited in the beginning and then drift off track. I noticed this with my clients who wouldn't get all their personal report remedies in, they would get distracted and then not have as good results as other members. So we started an amazing thread each week in our community - Win's Friday. It has been amazing to witness what's happening each week for our clients big and small wins but also for those who have drifted off track they see the results and it gives them a boost to take action again.

Accountability

Doing Feng Shui alone can be lonely and isolating. Not having anyone to bounce ideas off or get feedback. I know that's why when we created the PowerHouse Community to support our members made a phenomenal difference. Yes everyone's home is different and their personal reports are different but knowing you have a space to ask questions like - *what did you do?* has been incredible. I also love seeing people's creativity when it comes to implementation of their personal reports - it blows my mind and gives me loads of ideas too.

You might not be *afraid* of doing Feng Shui, but you might experience something else: indifference, boredom. You might shrug it off. You might think it won't work. Why? Why aren't you willing to give this a go? If it would bring you more clients and change others' lives for the better, why wouldn't you implement Feng Shui? Get honest with yourself about that and you might see where you are holding yourself back in business.

Naysayers

We all get them in business. People make hurtful remarks. They tell you how to run your business, even if they've never run one themselves. Learning detachment from these types of people who take their bad days or experiences out on you is so important.

One little trick I've learnt is to put the troublemaker's name in the freezer. You just write their name on a piece of paper and stick it in the freezer where they can chill out!

Naysayers may tell you that Feng Shui isn't a logical investment. You may be told you need to hire another coach or invest in a more business-focused course, funnels or Facebook ads to help your business. Again, if your environment isn't supportive, those things are only going to move the needle so far, particularly if your home is bad for money. Feng Shui isn't a 'nice-to-have'. It makes a fundamental shift in the foundation of your home and energy to allow everything else in your life to run smoother. This is exactly why Feng Shui needs to be a priority!

So many PowerHouse clients have gone on to say the naysayers in their lives changed their minds once they saw the Feng Shui begin to work. Let the results of Feng Shui — on your life and your business — do all the speaking for you. Then detach, detach, detach.

Failing to celebrate

I used to be useless at celebrating. I bet you weren't planning on celebrating any of the little wins that came through from Feng Shui, were you?

It's important to schedule this in. If it's your business, buy something to celebrate your launch or successful sale. Running a business is the greatest personal growth mechanism you can ever have. It will challenge you more than anything else. Feng Shui is all about the flow — so get on that party boat when things do seem to be going your way!

There are so many facets of Feng Shui, I could never cover them all in one book. Luckily, I have a tonne more free resources for you if you want to take Feng Shui further, including:

Finding out the energy of your home: **www.patricialohan.com/quiz**

And of course, you are always welcome to come and join us in the PowerHouse community. We have so many entrepreneurs in there who Feng Shui their homes, offices, shops, Airbnbs — you name it! Surrounding yourself with that kind of support is invaluable when you're just getting started. Plus, if you join PowerHouse, you'll get your own personalised report, making it even easier to get specific detailed remedies for your life and your business.

ELAINE'S STORY:

"IT'S JUST CRAZY HOW MUCH EASIER LIFE HAS BECOME."

I'm a single mother of a special needs daughter and life has been a battle for me. I didn't want to join PowerHouse, but I felt I had no other option. I'm kind of a busy person who likes to be moving around doing things, so I don't like doing programmes that require a lot of meditation; it makes me feel like I'm failing. I was nervous too, because it's an investment. I wasn't sure if this was something that I would start and stop or wouldn't have much value.

When I jumped in, there was oodles of content that was easy to digest. So much great stuff! I love the community. Everyone is super helpful, supportive, kind and loving. That energy alone elevated me and I found it so much fun. Now, when I'm cleaning my house or reorganising or decluttering, it's done with purpose and it is so much easier than it used to be for that reason.

I'm a recruiter and I have more clients and more jobs than I've ever had before. The referrals are coming thick and fast. The mum of my daughter's friend talked to me one day and handed me two new jobs from the HR director at her company the next. I've known this woman for 10 years, but as soon as I joined PowerHouse, this happened! The beautiful part is you don't have to understand it to go with the flow and be appreciative of all the wonderful things it brings.

Not only is my business easier, but everything seems to be falling into place better. I'm not always asking someone for advice anymore. I'm not trying to figure out who the best person is to talk to about this or that. I just know what to do and where to go and then the resources start coming in. I have this awesome new summer intern and a business advisor joined me out of the blue. It's just crazy how much easier life has become.

CHAPTER TWENTY-THREE

WHEN IT LOOKS LIKE IT'S NOT WORKING

One of the things that Feng Shui experts won't tell you is that your house can sabotage your success no matter how hard you try. This is because your house can be a particular shape, a particular type or in a lock. If you've implemented everything in this book and nothing seems to be working for your business, it could be down to the shape, type or potential money lock. Let's take a brief look at that now.

Like every person has their own unique fingerprint, every home has its own unique energetic blueprint. Your home is one-of-a-kind, with a personality, history and imprint on the world. You may be able to apply changes that are generally good for your home, yet the complexity of Feng Shui means there comes a time when your home requires some fine-tuning to find the exact combination it needs.

To harness the full potential of the energy of your home and the impact it has on your business, you will benefit most from a deeper level of Feng Shui. This deeper level is far beyond what I can teach in a book. In fact, it is far beyond the scope of any book. To experience this, you need personalised attention, starting with assessing how your home is doing. In other words, with all the changes you've been making, what has worked and where are you still stuck?

House shapes

Something often-overlooked in Feng Shui is house shape. As I mentioned earlier, an ideal house shape in Feng Shui is rectangular. Yes, this can be a bit boring but the energy moves around it smoothly! Houses that are crazy shapes can mean the energy runs erratically. Also, if you're 'missing' part of a Power Centre, you might not be tackling it in the best way. This often happens when people search online for Feng Shui fixes and find conflicting or cookie-cutter advice, because they don't understand that there are many different schools of Feng Shui. This leads to guesswork, which can cause havoc!

This happened to a client of ours before she worked with us. She mistook her family area for her wealth area. For five years, she'd been living in her house and hadn't spoken to her family. Luckily, when we gave her a personalised report and she implemented our suggestions, her dad called her out of the blue the next day!

It's these recommendations that are specific to every house. If you're reading this and thinking something is missing and the change you make doesn't seem to be working, it might be time to get a professional eye on it. Getting an expert allows you to make sure you're treating the shape properly.

House types

One element of Feng Shui which blows my mind is that your house is one of four types:

1. Good for People and Good for Money
2. Good for People and Bad for Money
3. Bad for People and Good for Money
4. Bad for People and Bad for Money.

Whichever your house is, it's directly impacting what is going on in your life — and especially your business life if you're working from home. So, how do you find out which house type yours is? Is your home good for people but bad for money? Have you welcomed financial abundance but seen your relationships take a nose-dive or simply stagnate? Is your house a money magnet or money repellent? Is your house a supportive home for loved ones or an unsupportive home for your business? Find out your house type by answering yes or no to these quick quiz questions below.

POWERHOUSE PRACTICE:
Complete the house type quiz

Check out the quiz at **www.patricialohan.com/quiz**

Money

1. Does money flow easily into your home/business?
2. Do you have a healthy savings account?
3. Can you always afford the things you want?
4. Since you moved into this house, have your finances improved?
5. Does your home/office feel luxurious and first class?
6. Have you had any unexpected financial windfalls?
7. Can you pay all your household bills with ease?

If you responded mostly yes, your house is good for money. If you answered mostly no, it's bad for money.

People

1. Do your spirits fall when you walk into your home/office?
2. Is there constant bickering and arguments in your home or business?
3. Do things break regularly?
4. Do you feel unsupported by your home or business?
5. Do you sometimes feel like you are jinxed, and that unexpected negative things happen out of the blue?

6. Have you experienced any, or all, of the following: legal suits, addictive behaviour, robbery, leaks?
7. Are unexpected accidents and illnesses a regular occurrence in your home or business?
8. Have you lost clients overnight?

If you answered mostly yes, your home is bad for people. If you had mostly no, it's good for people.

So, which house type are you currently in?

Good for People – Good for Money

This is the very first house type that we all would love to have. I'm sure you can think of someone who just seems lucky! They have the nice house, the nice car, the perfect relationship, their business is thriving. It could be all of these things or only one of these things.

If a house is Good for People — Good for Money, it doesn't mean life is perfect. But it does mean life can be pretty good and things genuinely seem to go your way if you're in one of these houses.

Of course, there could be things that are still stopping the flow. For example, Ken and I had a Good for People — Good for Money House but our front door faced our back door so money flowed in and then flowed right back out again and we went into a money lock. Little things like this can be caught on a personalised report and suggestions given to change it.

For now, you can start with the layers of Feng Shui we've talked about in the book, personalising the changes you make and setting intentions that are perfect for you. If you do this, you should start to see that good fortune flows even more freely. But there's always room for improvement, right?

Good for People – Bad for Money

When I think of this home, I always think of my client Carrie. She definitely had this type of house. Everyone in her family got on, they were well-balanced and just such a happy little family, always perfectly healthy. But it was like there was a leak in her bank account.

Carrie told me how she'd landed this amazing contract for over $28,000 and then two weeks later the plumbing in her entire house imploded. The cost to fix it? $28,000! If you experience money coming in and rushing out like this, it could be a huge sign that your house is bad for money and good for people. Don't panic. You can turn your money luck around with Feng Shui!

Bad for People – Good for Money

With this house type, there's a flow of money coming in but people don't stick around. What does that look like in a home? Well, it could mean arguing or bickering, whether with your partner, between your kids or with business people. It could look like lawsuits or problems with clients. It could even look like illness or health which affects your ability to run your business. Even though it's good for money, if you're sick or not as vibrant and healthy as you could possibly be, this could have a knock-on effect on your finances.

I'm sure you can think of someone in your life who does quite well for themselves but their life always seems to involve drama. If so, it's likely they're living in this type of house. As the old saying goes 'money doesn't buy happiness'. It's great to have abundance, but it's not all rosy in the house if people don't get on when you are at home.

If you have one of these houses, don't worry. The crazy stuff going on isn't your fault and it can be turned around.

Bad for People – Bad for Money

This is definitely the trickiest house type to have, but the good news it is changeable! If money is always tight, there's always drama, know that it doesn't have to stay that way and you don't have to move home. I've had countless clients who have had this type of house and we've turned it around.

The important part is about awareness and realising what is beyond your control. Houses do have personalities that can hold us back and impact our health, finances and relationships, both personally and professionally, but it can be changed!

Having this house type is such a huge opportunity for you because you now have the awareness that any crap stuff going on in your life is not your fault. The house you are living in could be causing many negative experiences to happen. And now you know about it, you can do something about it. The good news is that you can transform this space into somewhere much happier and luckier.

POWERHOUSE PRACTICE:
Find your type

Do the quiz and find out what your house type is. Now check in with that. Does it make sense? How does it make you feel? On a scale of 1 to 10, how ready are you to improve it?

There aren't specific identifiers I can share with you here because every house manifests differently. Like when you go for acupuncture, an acupuncturist isn't going to treat any two people the same, even if they have the same conditions because it depends on their history, other symptoms and what is going on in their life. Your house is the same.

The questions you have just answered can be used as an indicator of the type of house you live in, but a deeper analysis of your exact house type will be required when you go to the next level of personalisation, where I highly recommend the involvement of a trained professional.

Whatever your house type, know that right now you have the opportunity to turn around your fortune and improve the flow of prosperity and happy people in your business and in your life. With the power of Feng Shui, any and every house can become good for both money and people.

Money locks

A money lock creates issues around money in the household. Think: money drama! I've mentioned money locks a few times and I admit they sound pretty daunting! Before we get to what you can do about them, know that there's no real reason why they happen. It's just the energy moving in the house. If house shapes are like our body shapes, and house types are like our personalities, then money locks are just when your house is down on its luck.

Money locks can run on a one-year or a twenty-year cycle. Even if your house is good for money, it can go into a lock! It's just one of those tough periods that people often don't realise until they look back.

One client had a house that was good for people, good for money, but it was in a twenty-year money lock. The people who had lived there before her had had loads of financial issues and there had been a lot of paperwork and money issues to even buy the house. When my client moved in, her money situation wasn't great. Luckily, when I worked with her in PowerHouse to release the lock, she got these amazing windfalls of money for her family, like insurance refunds, mortgage rebates, pay rises. It was like the floodgates opened!

If you think you are in a money lock, the good news is it can be unlocked! This is the power of Feng Shui. It can help prevent things from unfolding that we don't want to see for ourselves.

Again, fixing a lock is personalised, so addressing this requires a professional to look over your home's unique blueprint to determine what to do about it. Professionals can even predict that it will happen in advance!

Where are you on the Wheel of Life?

As you can see, Feng Shui has a layering effect. There are many different factors that can influence what is happening in your home, your life and your business. For example, your house might be good for money but if your abundance area isn't there or it has bad energy, that might be why you're not experiencing a good money flow!

What we've been doing in this book is diving into the intentionality of setting up your space for success, but this is the tip of the iceberg when it comes to Feng Shui. Yes, setting up your environment is super important. Yes, knowing what each of the nine areas represents can help us be more intentional with our space. Yet underneath that is the energetics of it all, which is more than just where we position a desk or where we put a bowl of coins.

It's my belief that some part of us calls in our houses like a magnet. Those houses mirror our lives, our businesses, our work and our relationships back to us.

POWERHOUSE PRACTICE: Wheel of life

Take a minute to reflect on those nine areas of your life and business in terms of where you are *right now*. On a scale of 1 to 10 with 1 being awful and 10 being your dream life, what does each area feel like right now?

Download your own copy of this from **www.patricialohan.com/bizmiracles**

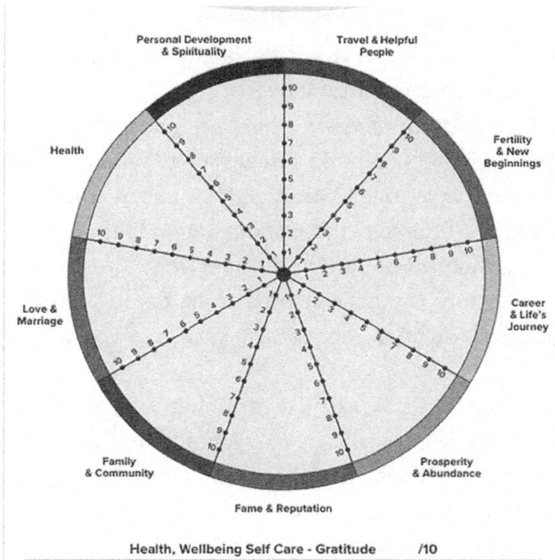

- **In your health area:** What is the overall health of your business? What is your own personal vitality like? Do you jump out of bed every morning excited to work?
- **In the career area:** How confident do you feel in your business mission? Does it feel like a job or does it feel like pure joy? That's the sign of a 10!
- **For the knowledge area:** Do you want to learn more in your field? Do you feel stuck or divinely guided? How deeply do you trust your intuition or do you feel like you don't know anything?
- **In teamwork and growth:** Do you like your team? If you don't have a team, do you feel supported? Do you eventually want a team?
- **For your prosperity:** Are your bills always covered? Is there always just enough or are you always dipping into savings or an overdraft? Is there always *more* than enough?
- **In the fame area:** Do people know of you? Know of your business? Could you be more well-known? If people were talking about you, would they be able to tell others what you do? Would it be the first thing they think of? Are you being recognised in your industry?

- **In business relationships:** How are your relationships with the people you work with? What are your interactions like with people in your community?
- **In the creativity section:** Where are you with creating? Do new ideas and offers come to you easily? Where are you with bringing new things to life? Are launches easy? Where are you with expressing yourself? In business and in life?
- **For the helpful people and travel area:** Does the perfect person arrive at the perfect time to help you with the thing you need help on? Are you globally known (if you want that)?

What would your life look like if everything was a 10? What would your business look like if it was a 10? What would your life feel like if everything was a 10? How would that impact you? How would it impact your clients or the work you do? How would it impact your family? Take a few minutes to journal on that now.

Back to your wheel. Circle those numbers on the wheel given to you above and then connect the dots. What shape does it make? If everything in your life was a 10, your shape would be a circle — a wheel.

When we have a balance of yin and yang, which is the purpose of Feng Shui, we move into the energy of flow and that's when things line up and start to happen all at once! You may feel lighter, happier, and life gets better, smoother. When you realise the impact that is having on your life, you notice the impact it is having on others too! Not just your clients and those you want to help, like we set out in your business mission at the start, but also your family and friends! That impact rebounds and abundance flows even more as a result of it. And *then* you are making a difference.

That is the journey of Feng Shui.

As a Feng Shui expert, I know which of the nine areas in your home are going to be off because of what's going on in your life. If your Wheel of Life shape is a square, or a keyhole, a balloon, a fried egg, it tells me exactly which part of your home isn't balanced. What's more, if I were to do your personalised Feng Shui report, where you provide answers to a detailed questionnaire, and we mapped the answers for your in a similar way to the exercise above, it would almost certainly match your Wheel of Life!

The benefit of the personalised report is that I can then look and say, "Well, this is why your kids are fighting. It's not because they're bad kids but because the energy in your relationships area is so low it's causing friction. Here's how we can improve that."

The energy of each of your nine areas might be invisible, but what is happening in your life shows the impact each area is having on you, your life and the lives of your family, as well as your business. These are not beyond your control because you can change them!

I hope you've already seen results coming in for your business through the changes you've implemented as you've worked through this book. If you haven't, don't worry. You haven't been doing it wrong! It might be that an area of your home is missing, your house type might need a specific remedy, or you may have a lock that requires a deeper Feng Shui approach. All of these things can be easily addressed, and in fact, are addressed in our PowerHouse programme.

You've heard from plenty of testimonials of PowerHouse members now and many of them have had houses that are bad for money, bad for people or bad for both! They've still gone on to have incredible success, even windfalls, in their home lives and their businesses. If you feel like PowerHouse is the next step you need on your Feng Shui journey, you can find out more here: https://patricialohan.com/powerhouse.

Chapter Twenty-Four

MY WISH FOR YOU

My wish for you is that you become a PowerHouse in Business with Feng Shui. That your business flourishes and you flourish alongside it. For you to be living your dreams awake making the impact you so truly desire to do so. For your entire home and workspace to be supporting you in every aspect of your life. So that you can flourish, grow, shine your light brightly and be the divine, beautiful being that you are meant to be. That your work life and business feels smooth and your business is easy and joyful.

I want you to work in business and live in a home where your spirit rises when you walk in. A space you feel totally supported by, that you feel aligned to its environment, and that there's a daily sense of tapping into flow.

Chapter Twenty-Five

YOUR MARCHING ORDERS

Well, that's it! That's everything you need to know about getting started with Feng Shui for your business. From its history to how I learnt about how to incorporate it into my business, from how to assess your own business to using the nine guas or Power Centres of Feng Shui. We started with decluttering to clear space in your business to make way for your new intentions. Then we learnt about the nine centres and how to find them in your office space. Whether you chose to do it for your whole home or just your office, I hope you are feeling clear about what Feng Shui steps to take. And if you've already started, maybe you're already feeling the effects of creating an intentional space for your business!

As you worked through each Power Centre in Part 3, you might also have started to take stock of where your business currently is and where you want it to go in the future. From your business mission to your vision board to implementing the enhancements, keep up this practice that everything you want can come true. My business is living proof!

Whatever stage of business you are in, my wish is that you've found the business insights useful, and now have a clear idea of what action points you are going to get done. It doesn't have to be done all at once.

Every action counts and each little shift leads you one step closer to the business of your dreams.

Now that you have a better understanding of what Feng Shui is, and what it isn't, you will begin to see the power of it as you take action. I hope you can see how simple it truly is to set up a space with intention and that you continue the practice as your results come in.

So, what do you do next? If I had to break down your to-do list into four fundamentals, it would be this. Firstly, figure out where the Power Centre areas are in your space. Secondly, write those affirmations! I know I've suggested that you place your affirmations somewhere you can see them, but you are free to keep them somewhere private too. Especially if you think anyone in your life might laugh or judge you, let those intentions begin to seed before people go stomping all over them. Thirdly, visualise! Get into that vibrational state of where you want your business to be and the results have to come when you're working in alignment. Finally, show up. For yourself, for your business, for your space.

With that in mind, I want to finish off by sharing my last little pieces of business advice I wish I had known at the beginning of my journey, and the framework that has served me well.

Let's start with showing up. The Universe rewards you for showing up. When I was hustling in those early days selling incense and singing bowls, I got their email address too. Because if they got a singing bowl off me, they more than likely would have liked to come to a sound bath. Doing this was vital.

Remember that there are no right or wrong ways to build your business. There are just lessons and successes. When you look back, you will love the journey for what it was. It's not about hustle and burnout. It's okay to let your business be easy and filled with joy. Don't be afraid to stand out.

Show up and be in the flow, stay in your lane, whatever that means to you. Whether that's in person or online. Whether you are starting from zero or already running a six-figure business. Trust yourself. Back yourself. Move with intention. Because it's your energy that drives your business. Don't forget to tend to it first.

And don't forget to leave some space for magic. Consistently showing up with intention will do most of the work for you, but it's always nice when things you never expected happen too! You'll always be constantly figuring out your next best step. Business is like Feng Shui, a never-ending practice!

The *single biggest business sabotage* is an unsupportive environment. When you operate in an unsupportive workspace, it's like being in a cycle of one step forward and two steps back. That energy is blocking you from getting to the next level that you are working towards — a sizzling business, a career that lights you up, harmonious relationships with clients and truly stepping into your life's purpose.

Thankfully, with the steps you've learnt here, you can begin to make that dream day you started journaling on at the beginning of this book a reality. If you're ready to take those dreams and 10X them for the exact same effort, it's time to place yourself in an environment that is going to support you in doing that. In PowerHouse, you get the opportunity to create a space that matches those big dreams and desires you have!

Just like in business, you can't do it alone and you'll go so much further with support and help. Inside this community, we can help you amplify that loving magnetic energy for every action you take so that *everything* you want can come towards you — while allowing what you don't want to fall away.

You could be like Emma, who dedicated every week to the programme and then got featured on the front of national papers for campaigns she was passionate about. You could be like Tonya, who went from never being on TV to being on it 14 times in one year. Not only that but her kids are doing better and even her husband loves it.

You could even choose to do PowerHouse with your partner. Rachel and David embarked on their Feng Shui journey as a couple and their results are an example of the kind of magic that can happen. David made five figures off his first ebook and audiobook, and booked out months in advance in his business. His company thrived so much that he told Rachel she didn't have to work anymore. For the first time in their lives together, both of them were able to focus on themselves and meet their own needs.

That's the beauty of PowerHouse and Feng Shui. You've heard the testimonials in here, the magic that happens and the results that speak for themselves. I hope you've realised by now that this isn't just a book on how to Feng Shui your office — but a guide on how to completely change your life and that of your loved ones. Those big dreams you have? That magic you're putting into place with these changes? That's going to spill out and affect everyone in your household and anyone who comes into your energy.

People in PowerHouse frequently tell me of windfalls for their partners, good things happening for their kids, and businesses exploding in growth. That big dream you had at the beginning? I'm not here to tell you it could come true. I'm telling you it *will* come true if you're willing to do the work and put yourself in the right supportive environment that can assist your energy. My business and those of my PowerHouse clients are a testament to that.

Imagine waking up and having to only work for an hour a day on a business you love, and being able to let a team you love take care of the rest. Imagine starting your morning doing yoga and going for a massage, while money still rolls into your business. Imagine being featured on the cover of *Forbes*, or your kids getting better grades, or your spouse coming home with an unexpected pay rise. Imagine being debt-free, mortgage-free, and owning your own dream home. Imagine being able to retire your partner. These are all things that *have* been done in PowerHouse.

This is why I love being able to share the power of Feng Shui with others. I'm so excited that you're able to begin this journey now and have your home/office support you as you begin to build the life of your dreams with effortless success. I'd love to hear of any successes you've already had with this book! Feel free to either leave a review of this book and share your results or join me on one of my social media channels or email newsletter. I'll leave my links below for you.

There's an amazing opportunity for you to come and join us at the next level when you're ready. Honestly, your house doesn't have to be fancy to get started. It's all about getting those nine areas of your life in alignment. When we see that in our PowerHouse clients, that's when those success stories come through.

The PowerHouse programme is a beautiful journey. That's the only word I can use to describe it — a journey. You'll join an incredible community, have all your questions answered individually, get the chance to submit your information in a step-by-step guide for a personalised Feng Shui report, and receive all the how-to videos to support you as you take your Feng Shui practice to a deeper level. This report will tell you what your house type is, how to balance it, and some simple things you can put in immediately that are specific to your home to get the energy moving. We do your floor plan for you and tell you exactly where each area is and what personal remedy will work.

When you put these remedies in, your house won't look any different, but your life will! Your business will, your bank account will, and your relationships certainly will.

You'll find everything you need to come and join us at
https://patricialohan.com/powerhouse

ABOUT THE AUTHOR

Patricia Lohan is the international best-selling author of *The Happy Home: Your Guide To Creating A Happy, Healthy, Wealthy Life.* Patricia Lohan helps women make their homes magnetic to money, luck, and blessings. She shows you what they don't teach in schools, what lies between the lines, and what her top-secret tools are for success. She is a Feng Shui expert, a healer, and a passionate female entrepreneur who has shaped her dream life, living between Bali, Greece, Italy and Ireland with her husband and Toby (the cutest Bischon Frise ever). Patricia has a gift for making Feng Shui simple and easy to understand and implement.

She has helped thousands of people across the globe embrace Feng Shui and creates lasting changes in their homes, lives, and businesses. Patricia has seen first-hand the power of the mind, surroundings, and inner-healing, clearing and aligning everything so it works holistically.

Follow her on Instagram
www.instagram.com/powerhousefengshui
www.instagram.com/patricialohan_

ACKNOWLEDGEMENTS

As I taught and shared my passion for Feng Shui, more and more people said I should write a book and I did all about the home, then more and more entrepreneurs came into my world asking questions about how Feng Shui could help them flourish too. Thank you to all of you for requesting this book.

You know who you are.

I am SO excited for people to embrace Feng Shui, something that has totally transformed my life for the better, and that of the thousands of women I have supported in my PowerHouse course and through my free training programmes.

Thank you to my family and friends for your continued support and encouragement.

Thank you to all my clients and the participants of PowerHouse — it's your incredible success stories, transformations, and dedication to creating a better life that spurs me on every day.

To all my teachers and mentors. To my incredible team who have facilitated all my crazy ideas and help me get Feng Shui out into the world every day.

I am SO grateful for my biggest personal Feng Shui success; meeting my amazing husband, Ken who has tirelessly supported me on this journey in life, love and business. I LOVE our adventures together and how, one house at a time, we are changing the world for the better. And of course Toby, thank you for your big kisses, cuddles unconditional love.

Printed in Great Britain
by Amazon

45467357R00145